THOUGHTS ON POPERY

by
Rev. William Nevins, D. D.
Late Pastor of a Church in Baltimore

sola fide
PUBLISHERS

www.solafidepublishers.com

Thoughts on Popery
by Rev. William Nevins

Originally Published in 1836
by John S. Taylor, Brick Church Chapel
New York

Reprint Edition © 2014
Sola Fide Publishers
Post Office Box 353
Clayton, Georgia 30525
www.solafidepublishers.com

Cover and Interior Design by
Magnolia Graphic Design

ISBN-13: 978-0692346099
ISBN-10: 0692346090

PREFACE

The lamented author of the following articles had long mourned over the influence of Romanism, as essentially a political rather than a *religious* institution – attracting men by its splendid and imposing *exterior*, to the neglect of that *spirituality of heart*, without which no man can "see the kingdom of God." He had made repeated endeavors to engage what he considered abler pens in exposing its absurdities; and at length, as a means of reaching the greatest number of minds, commenced the insertion of brief miscellaneous articles bearing on the subject in a widely circulated weekly newspaper the New York *Observer* using the signature M. S. – the finals of his name. In familiarity of style, kindness and cheerfulness of manner, and plain common sense, they are adapted to secure the attention and carry conviction to the heart of the general reader; while their richness of thought and clearness and conclusiveness of argument will render them not less acceptable to mature and cultivated minds. Finding the reception they met, it was the design of the author to comply with requests from numerous sources entitled to his regard, by himself (when the series should have been somewhat further extended) embodying them in a volume; but the failure of his health and the early close of his valuable life prevented the fulfillment of that design. They are now given to the public in accordance with general suggestion of the author, but essen-

3

ions of the author, but essentially in the form in which they at first appeared.

CONTENTS

CHAPTER ONE
The Sufficiency of the Bible as a Rule of Faith and Guide to Salvation

This is the great matter in controversy between Protestants and Roman Catholics. *We* say the Bible is sufficient. *They* say that it is not. Now, suppose that Paul the apostle be permitted to decide between us. We are agreed to refer the matter to him. Can our opponents object to this reference? Let Paul then be consulted in the only way in which he can be, viz. through his acknowledged writings. It is agreed on all hands that he wrote the *second* epistle to Timothy. Well, in the *third* chapter of that epistle, and at the 15th verse, he writes to Timothy thus: "And that from a child thou hast known the Holy Scriptures, which are able to make thee wise unto salvation." That the Greek is here correctly translated into English, any scholar may see.

Here then we have what Paul *wrote*, and I cannot believe that he would *write*, in a letter to Timothy, that the Holy Scriptures are capable of being known by a child, and able to make wise unto salvation, and then say, to be handed down by tradition, that they are so obscure and abstruse that one can make nothing out of them.

But what did Paul write to Timothy about the Holy Scriptures? He reminds him that he had known them from a child, that is, he had been acquainted with them so far as to understand them from that early age. Now, either Timothy was a most extraordinary child, of which there is no proof, or else the Holy Scriptures of the Old Testament, and of the New, so far as the latter was written and recognized at the time, are intelligible to a child. I see not how this conclusion can in any way be evaded. If the child of Eunice could and did know them, why may not my child and your child, and any child of ordinary understanding? And what do we want more for a rule of faith, than a Bible which a child can understand? The Bible then cannot be insufficient as a rule of faith, through any want of *perspicuity* in it. That point is settled.

But Paul says something more to Timothy about these same Scriptures: *"which"* he says, *"are able to make thee wise unto salvation."* Why, what is the matter with the man? He talks as if he had taken lessons of Luther. When did he live? They say that the Protestant religion is only three hundred years old, but here is a man who lived well nigh eighteen hundred years ago, that writes amazingly like a Protestant about the Holy Scriptures. He says (and I have just been look-ing at the Greek to see if it is so there, and I find that it is) they are *able* to make thee *wise unto salvation.* Now, who wishes to be wiser than that? and if they can make *one* thus wise, they can make any number equally wise. So then the Scriptures can be known by children, and can make wise to salvation those who know them. This is Paul's decision, and here should be an end of the controversy. If this prove not the sufficiency of the Bible as a rule of faith and guide to salvation, I know not how anything can be proved. I will tell you what I am deter-mined to do the next time a Catholic opens his mouth to me about the insufficiency and obscurity of our rule of faith. I mean to take hold of the sword of the Spirit by this handle, 2 Tim. 3:15, and I mean to hold on to this weapon of heavenly temper, and to wield it manfully, until my opponent surrender or retreat. He cannot stand before it.

But before I close this, I must say, that if the Scriptures which existed when Paul wrote to Timothy were able to make wise unto salvation, how much more are they with what has been added to the canon since? And here, by the way, we have an answer to the question which the Catholic asks with such an air of triumph: "How, if this be your rule of faith, did Christians get along before the New Testament was written and received?" Very well; they had Scriptures enough to make them "wise unto salvation" as early as the time of Timothy; and they had, many years before that, all the Old Testament, and a part of the New. Now, with Moses and the prophets, and the Psalms, and Matthew's Gospel, and perhaps some others, together with a large number of divinely inspired men, I think they must have got along very comfortably.

One thing more I desire to say. It is this: that there is an advantage for understanding the Bible, which does not belong to any book whose author is not personally accessible. The advantage is, that we have daily and hourly opportunity to *consult the Author* of the Bible on the meaning of it. We can, at any moment we please, go and ask him to interpret to us any difficult passage. We can lift off our eyes from the word of truth, when something occurs which we do not readily comprehend, and direct them to the throne of grace. And what encouragement we have to do this! *James* tells us, "If any of you lack wisdom, let him ask of God, that giveth to all men liberally, and upbraideth not; and it shall be given him." So then we have the Bible to inform and guide us, and we have constant opportunities of consulting its Author in regard to its meaning. Is it not enough? I, for one, am satisfied. I can dispense with the fathers, &c. &c.

CHAPTER TWO
The Source of Heresies

The Roman Catholics say it is the Bible. They trace all the errors and divisions which prevail, to the Scriptures as their fountain. Do they know whose book it is which they thus accuse? How dare they charge God with being "the Author of confusion?" But is the Bible to blame for heresies? Christ gives a very different account of the matter. He says in Matt. 22:29, to the Sadducees, "Ye do err, not knowing the Scriptures." He makes *ignorance of the Scriptures* the source of heresies. He does not agree with the priests.

It is very strange, if the reading of the Scriptures is the cause of heresies in religion, that the Bereans, who *searched* them *daily*, because they would not take on trust even what *Paul* said (and I suspect they would not have treated *Peter* any more civilly), did not fall into any of these errors. It would seem to have had quite a contrary effect, for it is added, *"therefore* many of them believed." Acts 17:11-12. Whatever these Bereans were, it is clear that they were not good Catholics.

But after all it is not surprising that these noble Bereans did not fall into any fatal error by reason of reading the Scriptures, since Peter says of Paul's hardest parts, and most obscure passages, that they do nobody any harm, but such as are both "unlearned and unstable;" and that they do them no harm, except they *wrest* them, that is, do absolute violence to them. 2 Pet. 3:16.

CHAPTER THREE
Private Interpretation

It is known to everybody how strenuously the Catholics oppose the reading of the Bible, or rather, I should say, the reader exercising his mind on the Bible which he reads. He may *read* for himself, if he will only let the church *think* for him. He may have a New Testament, and he may turn to such a passage as John 3:16, "God so loved the world that he gave his only begotten Son," &c. or to that, Matt. 11:28, 30, "Come unto me, all ye that labor and are heavy laden, and I will give you rest," &c. and he may read the words, but then he must not attempt to put a meaning upon them, though it be very difficult to avoid attaching a sense to them, since they are quite as easy to be understood as they are to be read. But he must not do it. At his peril he must not. He is guilty of the crime of private interpretation, if he does. Before he pretends to understand those passages, he must inquire how the church has always interpreted them, and what the popes and general councils have thought about them, and how *all* the *fathers*, from Barnabas to Bernard, not one excepted, have understood them. Well, now, it strikes me as rather hard upon the poor sinner, that he should be made to go through this long and difficult process before he is permitted to admire the love of God in the gift of his Son, and before he can go to Jesus for rest. And somehow

I cannot help suspecting that it is not necessary to take this *circuitous* course, and that it is not so very great a sin when one reads such passages, to understand them according to the obvious import of their terms.

But the Catholic asks, "Does not Peter condemn private interpretation?" And they point us to his 2d Epistle, 1:20. "Knowing this first, that no prophecy of the Scripture is of any private interpretation." Now you must know that Catholics, though they have no great attachment to the Bible, are as glad as any people can be, when they can get hold of a passage of it, which seems to establish some tenet of theirs. And as only a very small portion of the Bible has even the *appearance* of favoring them, one may observe with what eagerness they seize upon, and with what tenacity they cling to the rare passages which seem to befriend their cause. Thus they do with this passage of Peter. They quote it with an air of triumph, and exultingly ask what Protestants can have to reply to it.

Now, in the name of Protestants, I will state in two or three particulars what we have to say in opposition to the Catholic inference from these words of Peter. We say that that passage does not make for the Catholic cause, *first*, because if the right of private judgment and private interpretation is taken away by it, as they affirm, yet it is taken away with respect to only a small part of the Bible, viz. the *prophetic* part. He does not say that any other part, the historical, the didactic, or the hortatory, is of private interpretation, but only the prophetic, that part in which something is *foretold*. He does not say *no Scripture*, but *"no prophecy* of the Scripture is of any private interpretation." Allowing then to the Catholic all which he contends for, we are left with by far the larger part of the Bible open to private interpretation. Peter restricts us only in the matter of *prophecy!*

But *secondly*, let me say, that to whatever the remark of the apostle has reference, it can easily be shown that it does not mean what the Catholic understands it to mean. This is evident from what follows it. I wish the reader would turn to the passage. He will perceive that Peter, having said that no prophecy of the Scripture is of any private interpretation, proceeds to assign the reason of that assertion, or rather, as I think, goes into a further and fuller explanation of what he had said: "For the prophecy came not in old time by the will of man [that is, it was not of human invention, it did not express the conjectures of men], but holy men of God spake as they were moved by the Holy Ghost." Now I would ask if this reason confirms the Catholic view of the passage? Is the fact that the Bible was written by men inspired of God to write it, any reason why it should not be of private interpretation? Does the circumstance that God gave them the thoughts, and even suggested to them the words in which they should clothe them, render the production so unintelligible, or so equivocal in its meaning, that a private individual cannot be trusted to read it? That would be to say that God cannot make himself understood as easily as men can! The Catholic argument from this passage may be stated thus: *the Bible is an inspired book, therefore too obscure and ambiguous to be of private interpretation! Inspired, therefore unintelligible!*

If it be so hard to understand what God says, how was the divine Savior able to make himself understood by the common people who heard him gladly? I suspect they knew what he meant when he said, "Come unto me, and I will give you rest." The sermon on the mount seems to have been understood by those who heard it. No one thought of asking how others understood it. No one felt the necessity of an interpreter: everyone exercised his private judgment on what Christ said. Now, suppose that what Jesus said to the people, and they found no difficulty in understanding it, had been taken down in writing at the time, would not they who understood it when they *heard* it, have equally understood it when they *read* it? The *spoken* discourses of Christ were intelligible; have they become unintelligible by being *written?*

To return for a moment to the passage in Peter. I consider that the word rendered in verse 20, *interpretation*, should be translated as Dr. M'Knight translates it, *invention*; or, as another renders it, *impulse*: and verse 21 should be considered as explanatory of that which precedes it. If the apostle really intended to deny the right of private judgment, why does he in verse 19 exhort all the saints, to whom he wrote, to *take heed* to "the more sure word of prophecy," the very thing in reference to which he is supposed to deny the right of private judgment? Why should they *take* heed to it, if it is not of private interpretation? and why does he speak of it as "a *light* that shineth in a dark place?"

Finally, if no part of Scripture is of private interpretation, then of course the passage of Scripture, 2 Pet. 1:20, is not of private interpretation; and yet the Catholic exercises his private judgment upon it, and submits it to the private judgment of the Protestant, in the hope thereby of making him a Catholic! No part of Scripture, according to him, may be privately interpreted, but that which affirms that *no part, not even itself,* may be privately interpreted!

CHAPTER FOUR
Popery Unscriptural

———◈———

I undertake to prove that the Roman Catholic religion is *unscriptural* – that it is not borne out by the Bible. If I can do that, I shall be satisfied; for a religion, professing to be Christianity, which does not agree with the statements of Matthew, Mark, Luke, John, Paul, *Peter*, James and Jude, will, I am persuaded, never go down in the United States of America. It may do for Spain, Portugal and Italy; but it will not do here. There is too much respect for the Bible in this republican land to admit of such a thing. Republicans know too well how much liberty owes to the Bible. They know that tyranny cannot exist where the Bible, God's *magna charta* to mankind, is in the hands of the people. Besides, the people of this country have too much good common sense to take that for Christianity about which the evangelists and the apostles knew nothing. I think, therefore, that I shall have gained the point, if I show that Romanism and the Bible are at odds. This, if I mistake not, I can easily do.

Roman Catholics act very much as if they themselves did not regard their religion as being *scriptural*. Why, if they believe that their religion is the religion of the Bible, do they not put the Bible into the hands of the people, and advise them to read it, that they may become, or continue to be good Roman Catholics? Why not circulate far and wide the book which contains their religion? They need not take our translation of it. They have one of their own – the Douay. Let them circulate that. Why do they leave the whole business of distributing the Scriptures to the Protestants? Above all, why do they oppose the operations of Bible Societies, when they are only multiplying and diffusing copies of the book which contains the Roman Catholic religion?

I am particularly surprised that the Roman Catholics are not more anxious to put into general circulation the two epistles of *their* St. Peter, who they assert was the first Bishop of Rome, and earliest Pope. They acknowledge that he wrote two epistles, and that they are extant. Why, in the name of common sense, do they not let every Catholic have them! I do not wonder that they wish to keep out of sight of the people the epistles of Paul, who says, Gal. 2:11, that he withstood Peter to the face, "because he was to be blamed." Paul forgot at the moment that Peter was supreme and infallible! We are all liable to forget. But why the rulers of the church should be unwilling to let the people hear Peter, is the wonder with me. I have been reading his epistles, to see if I can discover why the Catholics are not friendly to their circulation. Perhaps it is because in them he says nothing about *Rome*, unless by *Babylon*, 1 Pet. 5:13, he means Rome, as John does in the Revelation: and never a word about his being Bishop of Rome, or Pope! The man seems to have no idea that he was a pope. He says in his 1st Epistle, 5:1, "The elders which are among you I exhort, *who am also an elder.*" An elder! was that all? Why, Peter, do you forget yourself? Do you not know that you are *universal Bishop, Primate of the Apostolical College, Supreme and Infallible Head of the Church?* He seems never to have known one word about it. Now I think I have hit upon one reason why it is thought best that the people in general should not be familiar with the writings of Peter.

I wish, for my part, that the Catholics would print an edition of Peter's Epistles, and give them general circulation among their members; for if the religion of these epistles is their religion I have no further controversy with them.

CHAPTER FIVE
The Evil of Believing Too Much

———◆◇◆———

It is a common saying among the Catholics, that it is better to believe too much than to believe too little; and it is one of the arguments with which they endeavor to make proselytes, that they believe all that Protestants believe, besides a good deal that Protestants do not believe. Hence they would have it inferred that their religion possesses all the advantages which belong to Protestantism, and some more into the bargain; so that if the religion of the Reformation is safe, much more is that of the church of Rome safe. Now, as I am certain that this way of *talking* (*reasoning* it is not worthy to be called) has some influence in making Catholics, I shall take the liberty of examining it.

Why is it better to believe too much than to believe too little? *Excess* in other things is not better than *defect*. To *eat* or *drink* too much is not better than to eat or drink too little. To believe that two and two make five, is as bad as to believe that two and two make three. One of these errors will derange a man's calculations as much as the other. The man who believes that two and two make five, has no advantage because he believes the whole truth and a little more.

A certain writer, who ought to be in high authority at Rome as well as everywhere else, represents additions to the truth to be as injurious and as offensive to God as subtraction from it. Rev. 22:18-19. "If any man shall add unto these things, God shall *add* unto him the plagues that are written in this book." Here you see what a man gets by believing too much. It is not altogether so safe a thing as the Catholics represent it to be. Adding is as bad as taking away. For every article added there is a *plague* added.

I suppose that one reason why these additions to the truth are so offensive to God is, that they are such additions as *take from* that to which they are added; just as when a man puts "a piece of new cloth into an old garment, that which is put in to fill it up taketh from the garment, and the rent is made worse." Mat. 9:16. All the additions of the church of Rome to Christianity take away from some of its doctrines. She first cuts a hole in the robe of Christ and then applies her patch! In order to make room for her doctrine of human merit, she has to take away just so much from the merit of Christ. The Protestant doctrine is, that we are justified by faith alone, without the deeds of the law. Nay, says the Catholic, our own good works have something to do in the matter of our justification. Now, this addition does not leave entire that to which it is added, but takes from it!

We hold to the *perfection* of the one sacrifice offered by Christ on the cross. The Catholics add to this the sacrifice of the mass. They are not satisfied with Christ's being *"once* offered to bear the sins of many," but they teach the strange doctrine that Christ is offered as often as a priest is pleased to say mass!

Nothing is farther from the truth than that the Catholic believes all which the Protestant believes, besides a great deal that the Protestant does not believe. The latter part of the assertion is correct. The Catholics believe a great deal which the Protestants do not. In the *quantity* of their faith they far surpass us. There is the whole that is comprehended in *tradition*. They believe every word of it – while Protestants are satisfied with Holy Scripture. But the Catholics do not believe all that Protestants believe; they do not believe the Protestant doctrine of regeneration, or justification, or other cardinal doctrines.

But, asks one, is not all that Protestants believe contained in the Scriptures! Yes. Well, Catholics believe the Scriptures. Therefore they believe all which Protestants do; and then, moreover, they believe tradition; so that they believe all which Protestants believe, and some more besides. Very logical, to be sure! But suppose that tradition and Scripture happen to contradict each other, how then? What sort of an addition to a testimony is a contradiction of it? I might give some precious specimens of these contradictions. The Catholic believes with Scripture, that "marriage is *honorable* in all;" and he believes with tradition, that it is *very disgraceful* in some. One of his rules of faith affirms that "all our righteousnesses are as filthy rags," but the other assures him that there is merit in his good works. One says that Peter was *to be blamed*, but the other asserts his infallibility. According to one, Peter was a simple *elder*; but according to the other, universal bishop, &c. The Catholic says he believes both, and therefore he is in a safer state than the Protestant. Well, when I can be convinced that two contradictory assertions are both true, I may believe as much as the Catholic believes. Meanwhile I am satisfied with believing enough; and not caring to be more than perfectly safe, I shall continue to be a Protestant.

CHAPTER SIX
The Nine Commandments

———❖———

"Nine commandments! What does that mean? I always thought the commandments were *ten.*" There used to be that number. There were ten proclaimed by the voice of God from Mount Sinai; and ten were written by the finger of God on the tables of stone, and when the tables were renewed, there were still ten: and the Jews, the keepers of the Old Testament Scriptures, always recognized ten; and so did the primitive church, and so do all Protestants in their creeds and catechisms. But the Roman Catholics (you know they can take liberties, for they are the true church, they are infallible. A person, and so a church, which cannot possibly make a mistake, need not be very particular about what it does), these Christians who have their head away off at Rome, subtract one from the ten commandments; and you know if you take one from ten, only nine remain. So they have but nine commandments. Theirs is not a Decalogue, but a Nonalogue.

It is just so. When, many years ago, I first heard of it, I thought it was a slander of the Protestants. I said, "O, it cannot be that they have dared to meddle with God's ten commandments, and leave out one. They cannot have been guilty of such impiety. Why, it is just as if some impious Israelite had gone into the holy of holies, opened the ark of the covenant, and taking out the tables of stone, had, with some instrument of iron, obliterated one of the commands which the divine finger wrote on them." But then it struck me how improbable it was that such a story should ever have gained currency, unless there was some foundation for it. Who would ever have thought of charging Roman Catholics with suppressing one of the commandments, unless they had done it, or something like it?

So I thought I would inquire whether it was so or not; and I did, and found it to be a fact, and no slander. I saw with my own eyes the catechisms published under the sanction of bishops and archbishops, in which one of the commandments was omitted; and the reader may see the same thing in *The Manual of Catholic Piety*, printed no farther off than in Philadelphia. The list of the commandments runs thus:

1. I am the Lord thy God; thou shalt not have strange Gods before me.

2. Thou shalt not take the name of the Lord thy God in vain.

3. Remember the Sabbath day, &c.

The reader will see that the commandment which the Catholics leave out, as being grievous to them, is the second in the series. It is the one that forbids making graven images and likenesses of anything for worship. That is the one they don't like; and they don't like it, because they do like pictures and images in their churches. They say these things wonderfully tend to promote devotion, and so they do away that commandment of God! David says, "I esteem all thy precepts concerning all things to be right." But he was no Catholic.

Well, having got rid of the second, they call the third second, and our fourth they number third, and so on till they come to our tenth, which, according to their numbering, is the ninth. But as they don't like the sound of "the nine commandments," since the Bible speaks of "the ten commandments," Exod. 34:28; Deut. 4:13, and everybody has got used to the number ten, they must contrive to make out ten some how or other. And how do you think they do it? Why, they halve their ninth, and call the first part ninth, and the other tenth.

So they make out ten. In the *Philadelphia Manual*, corrected and approved by the Right Rev. Bishop Kenrick, it is put down thus: "9th. Thou shalt not covet thy neighbor's wife. 10th. Thou shalt not covet thy neighbor's goods." You see they make two of the commandments to relate to coveting. It is not very probable the Lord did so. I reckon they were not so numbered on the tables of stone. But you see it would never do to let that second commandment stand, and it would never do to have less than ten: so they were laid under a sort of necessity to do as they have done. But, after all, it is a bad job. It is not near so ingenious as many of the devices of Popery. After all is said and done, they have but nine commandments; for everybody knows that by dividing anything you get not two wholes, but two halves: there is but one whole after the division. And so the ninth commandment is but one commandment after they have divided it. If they were to quarter it they could not make any more of it. If the Catholics are bent on dividing the last of the commandments, they should call the first half, 8th, and the second half, 9th. That is what they ought to do. That would be acting honestly, for they know they have left out one of the Lord's ten. They know that the Lord gave ten commandments, and they acknowledge only nine of them. It is a mean device to divide one of the nine, and then say they acknowledge ten. The Catholics know that the commandments, as they are in many of their catechisms, are not as they were written with the finger of God on the tables of stone. They know that one is wanting, and why it is they know. They had better take care how they do such things, for the Lord is a jealous God.

Indeed the Catholics are sorry for what they have done in this matter. It has timed out a bad speculation. This reduction of the law of God one-tenth, has led to the opening of many eyes. They would never do the like again. And as a proof of their repentance, they have restored the second commandment in many cases: they can show you a great many catechisms and books in which it is found. I had supposed that the omission

existed now only in the catechisms published and used in
Ireland, until I heard of the *Philadelphia Manual*. They had
better repent thoroughly, and restore the commandment in all
their publications. And I think it would not be amiss for them
to confess that for once they have been fallible; that in the
matter of mutilating the Decalogue, they could, and did err. If
they will afford us that evidence of repentance, we will forgive them, and we will say no more about it. We know it is a
sore subject with them; they don't know how to get along
with it. When one asks them, "How came you to leave out the
second commandment?" if they say, "Why, we have not left
it out of all our books?" The other replies, "But why did you
leave it out of any?" and there the conversation ends. Echo is
the only respondent, and she but repeats the question, "Why?"

CHAPTER SEVEN
Catholic Hostility to the Bible

———◆◇◆———

I am not surprised that the Roman Catholics dislike the Bible, for very much the same reason that Ahab, king of Israel, disliked Micaiah, the prophet of the Lord. 1 Kings 22:8. It is hard not to contract a strong dislike to that which is for ever bearing testimony against one. To love an enemy is one of the most difficult attainments. Now, the Bible is all the time speaking against the Catholic religion, and prophesying not good, but evil of it, just as Micaiah did of Ahab. It is natural, therefore, that the Catholic should feel an aversion to the Bible. We ought not to expect anything else. But I am somewhat surprised that they do not take more pains to conceal their dislike of it, for it certainly does not look well that the church of God should fall out with the oracles of God. It has an ugly appearance, to say the least, to see the Christian church come out against the Christian Scriptures.

I wondered much, when, a few years ago, the Pope issued his encyclical letter, forbidding the use of the Bible in the vulgar tongue. It certainly looks bad that Christ should say, "Search the Scriptures;" and that the vicar of Christ should say, "No, you shall not even have them," It has very much the appearance of contradicting Christ: but appearances may deceive in this case, as in transubstantiation. But I must do the

Pope justice. He does not unconditionally forbid the use of the Bible, but only the use of it in the *vulgar* tongue. The Pope has no objection that a person should have the Bible, provided he has it in a language which he does not understand. The English Catholic may have a French Bible, and the devout Frenchman may make use of an English or Dutch Bible; or both may have a Latin Bible, provided they have not studied Latin. An acquaintance with the Latin makes it as vulgar a tongue as any other. I have thought it due to the Pope to say thus much in his favor. Far be it from him to forbid the use of the Bible, except in the vulgar tongue!

Another more recent fact has surprised me not a little that a student of Maynooth College, Ireland, named O'Beirne, should have been expelled that institution for persisting in reading the Bible! Expulsion is a pretty serious thing. That must be esteemed a heinous crime which is supposed to justify so severe a penalty. I cannot see anything so criminal in reading the Scriptures. I wonder if the reading of any other book is forbidden at Maynooth: I suspect not. The authorities at Maynooth must think the Bible the worst book in the world. A student of that college may read whatever is most offensive to purity and piety in the ancient classics, without any danger of expulsion; but if he reads the Bible he is dismissed with dishonor! But I suppose they will say, he was not expelled for reading the Scriptures, but for contempt of authority, in that, after being forbidden to read the Scriptures, he still persisted in reading them. That makes a difference I must confess: still the young man's case was a hard one. Christ told him not only to read, but to *search* the Scriptures: the authorities of the college told him he must not. His sin consisted in obeying Christ rather than the government of the college. I think it might have been set down as *venial*. They might have overlooked the fault of preferring Christ's authority to theirs. "When the Son of man shall come in his glory," I don't believe he will *expel* the young man for what he did, though the college bade him "depart."

I wonder, and have always wondered, that the Catholics,

in prohibiting the Scriptures, do not except St. Peter's Epistles. Was ever any Catholic forbidden to read the letters ofa
Pope? I believe not. But if good Catholics may, and should
read the "Encyclical Letters" of the Popes, why not let them
read the "General Epistles" of the first of Popes, Peter? Why
is it any more criminal to read the letters of Pope Peter, than
those of Pope Gregory? I cannot explain this.

Here is another fact that has surprised me. A recent
Galway newspaper denounces, by name, two Protestant cler-
gymen as *reptiles*, and advises that they should be at once
trampled on. What for? Why, for the sin of holding a Bible
meeting, and distributing the Scriptures! It speaks of them as
a hell-inspired junto of incarnate fiends, and says, "If the devil
himself came upon earth, he would assume no other garb than
that of one of these biblicals." The Irish editor adds, "The
biblical junto must be put down in Galway." He is evidently
in a passion with the Bible: I suppose it must be because it
prophecies no good of him. Certainly he cannot think the Bible very favorable to his religion, otherwise he would not
proclaim such a crusade against its distribution. It is the first
time I ever heard it asserted, that the managers and members
of Bible Societies are *ipso facto* incarnate fiends. It seems
singular, that those who promote the circulation of a *heaven-
inspired* volume, should be themselves, as a matter of course,
hell-inspired. I cannot think that Exeter Hall and Chatham-
street Chapel become *Pande-moniums* whenever the Bible
Society meets in them. Nor shall I believe that Satan is going
to turn Bible distributer, until I actually see him "walking
about" on this agency.

I do not know how it is, but I cannot help looking on the
circulation of the Scriptures as a benevolent business – the
gratuitous giving of the word of God to the children of men as
a good work. When recently I read an article stating that the
Young Men's New York Bible Society had undertaken to
supply the emigrants arriving at that port with the Bible in their
respective languages, I almost instinctively pronounced it
a good work; and I was astonished, as well as grieved, to find

that some of the emigrants refused to receive the volume. I
suppose that if the agent had offered them a volume of the
Spectator, or a novel, they would have taken that. Any book
of man they could have thankfully received; but the book of
God they had been instructed to refuse, should that be offered
them! The agent reports the following fact: "June 17, visited
on their landing a large number of emigrants from Ireland, not
one of whom could be prevailed on to receive a Bible, even as
a gift. One of the females told me, if I would give her one she
would take it with her and burn it." Who, do you suppose, put
them up to refuse the Bible? And who put it into the head of
the woman to speak of burning the Bible? I think any person,
in whatever part of the country born, could guess. I guess it
was not any infidel – I guess it was a priest.

But perhaps the reason they refused the Bibles offered
them, was, that they had other and better Bibles. That is not
pretended. They had none. Now, it seems to me they might
have accepted our Bibles until they could procure their own
better Bibles. An imperfectly translated Bible is better than
none: no translation of the Bible was ever so bad as to be worse
than no Bible. What if the Douay is before all other Bibles, yet
King James' may answer one's turn until he can get the Douay.
The Catholics complain that we give their people an errone-
ously translated Bible: why, then, do they not supply them with
a correct translation? When they undertake that, we will cease
to trouble them. We would be very glad to see every Catholic
family possessing, and capable of reading, the Douay Bible,
although it does make repentance towards God to consist in
doing penance appointed by men. But that they have no idea
of doing. Does not the Pope forbid the use of the Bible in the
vulgar tongue? I know many Catholics have it, but it is no part
of their religion to have a Bible. They get their Christianity
without the trouble of *searching* the Scriptures. Indeed they
would in vain search in the Scriptures for what they call Christianity. If they were not perfectly conscious that their religion
is not to be found in the Bible, do you suppose they would
denounce and persecute that book as they do? Would they di-

rect their inquiries to fathers, and councils, and priests for information, rather than to prophets, evangelists, and apostles?

CHAPTER EIGHT
Something For the Rev. Mr. H.

———◆❖◆———

Mr. H., the Goliath of the Catholics, seems to be very fond of asking questions which he thinks nobody can answer. I am not acquainted with any writer who makes more frequent use of the interrogation point. But his questions are not quite so unanswerable as he supposes. I will just answer two of the string of questions with which he commences a recent letter to Mr. B. and then I beg leave to ask a few.

He wants to know *first*, what the Protestant religion is. He has been often told, but I will tell him again. *It is the religion of the Bible.* It was not called *Protestant* when the Bible was written, for then there was no corruption of Christianity to *protest* against. But it is the same, however called. There it is, in the Bible. Read it. Read any part of it. You cannot go amiss to find *the religion of the Reformation* in the Bible. Read particularly the epistle to the Romans, to whom Catholics pretend to refer their origin; or the epistle to the Ephesians. I wonder if a passage from either of these prominent epistles was ever quoted by anyone in proof of any peculiarity of the Roman Catholic church! I suspect never. Protestants, however, make great use of them.

But, says the interrogator, "tell us what particular doctrines constitute the Protestant religion. Telling us it is the religion of the Bible, is telling us *where* it is, but not *what* it is."

And is it not enough to tell you *where* you may find a thing? Have you no *eyes?* Have you no *mind?* Do you want one to think for you? Is not that all which Jesus Christ did? He gave the Scriptures to the Jews, and said, "search them." So we put the Bible into your hand, and say, *there is our religion.* And yet you ask, "Where was your religion before Luther?" Before Luther! we tell you where it was before the earliest fathers. It was in the Gospels and Epistles, where it is now, and ever will be. What have we to do with Luther or Augustine, or any of them, until we get as far back into antiquity as St. John?

But Mr. H. asks again, "What society of Christians ever taught this pretended religion of Christ previous to the Reformation?" Why, Mr. H. do not affect such ignorance – you must be *joking*, when you ask such a question. Did you never hear of a society of Christians residing at Rome, some of whom were of Caesar's household, to whom one Paul wrote a letter, which has come down to us? Now, if it cannot be ascertained what that society of Christians "taught," yet it can easily be ascertained what *was taught* them. It is only to read the letter. And I think it not improbable that that society of Christians professed and taught what St. Paul taught them.

But there was another respectable society of Christians, a good while "previous to the Reformation," who seem to have known something about this "pretended religion of Christ," called Protestant. They dwelt in a city named Ephesus. That same Paul resided among them three years, preaching the Gospel, and he did it *faithfully*. He "shunned not to declare all the counsel of God." After establishing a flourishing church there, he went away, and subsequently addressed an epistle to them, which also has come down to us. In this epistle it is to be presumed that he embodied the substance of the Gospel, which he had taught them "publicly and from house to house." He is not to be suspected of *preaching* one thing and *writing* another. Will Mr. H. deny that the society of Christians at Ephesus professed and taught the doctrines of the epistle to the Ephesians?

I think not. Well, sir, what are the doctrines of that epistle? Are they yours or ours – Catholic or Protestant? I will leave it to any intelligent infidel on earth to decide. Will Mr. H. agree to the reference? O no, he wants us to leave it to a pope, and general council, and the *unanimous fathers*.

I have told Mr. H. now of two societies of Christians who "taught this pretended religion of Christ previous to the Reformation." I could tell of more; but two are enough. He only asked for *one*.

Now I would ask Mr. H. a question. Where was your religion, Mr. H. at the time the Bible was written? I am curious to know. How came the evangelists and apostles to know nothing about it, if it is really the religion of Christ? Perhaps Mr. H. can clear up this difficulty. I wish he would, if he can. I do not want him to say where his religion was *after* the Bible was written, and *after* all the evangelists and apostles were dead. I am informed on that point. I want to know where the Roman Catholic religion was *before* those good men died; where it was *before the fathers*.

They talk about the *antiquity* of the Roman Catholic religion. It is *old*, I must confess. It bears many marks of age upon it. But the difficulty is, it is *not old enough* by a century or two at least. They say it is the *first* form of Christianity. That is a mistake. It is the *second*. The first appeared for a while, then "fled into the wilderness, where she had a place prepared of God," and re-appeared at the Reformation. They call it a new religion. But no, it is *the old restored*. If anyone doubts the *identity* of the *restored* religion, let him but compare its features with that which appeared and flourished in the apostolic age.

Another question I beg leave to ask Mr. H. "Did the first Christians of Rome hold the doctrines contained in the epistle to the Romans, or did they not?" If they did not, they must have departed from the faith sooner than Paul predicted that they would. If they did hold the doctrines of the epistle, then, since these are the very doctrines which the friends of the Reormation contend for, have we not here the example of a society holding the doctrines of the Reformation long before the actual era of the Reformation? I have other questions to ask, but I wait for these to be answered.

CHAPTER NINE
Distinction of Sins Into Mortal and Venial

———◆◇◆———

I was not aware, until recently, that Roman Catholics of this age, and in this country, make that practical use which I find they do of the distinction of sins into *mortal* and *venial*. For the truth of the following narrative I can vouch. An intelligent gentleman being, a few weeks since, expostulated with by a Protestant lady, on his spending the whole of a certain Sabbath in playing cards, replied with the utmost readiness, and with every appearance of confidence in the validity of his apology, "O, that is not a *mortal* sin." Several similar examples of a resort to this distinction were reported to me. Now, can that system be the religion of Jesus Christ, which recognizes this horrible distinction, and puts such a plea as this into the mouth of a transgressor of one of the commandments of that Deca-logue which God's own voice articulated and his own finger wrote? I cannot express the feelings I have, when I think of the multitudes who are forming a character for eternity under the influence of doctrines like these. What sort of a character must they form!

How completely at variance with the Scriptures is this distinction! "Cursed is everyone that continueth not in all things which are written in the book of the law to do them – the wages of sin is death – the soul that sinneth, it shall die."

Gal. 3:10; Rom. 6:23; Ezek. 18:4. Is not all sin disobedience to God? and may he be disobeyed in any respect without guilt? Did ever a father of a family recognize such a distinction in the government of his children? Did Christ atone for what are called venial sins, or did he not? If he did not, then he did not atone for all sin. If he did atone for them, they must be worthy of death, since he died for them.

The truth is, all sin is mortal, if not repented of; and all sin is venial, that is, pardonable, if repented of. There is no sin which the blood of Christ cannot cleanse from. And nothing but *that* can take out any sin.

It is not worth while to reason against such a distinction. I only mention it as one of the absurd and pernicious errors of the system to which it belongs.

CHAPTER TEN
The Deadly Sins

In *The Christian's Guide to Heaven* I read with some interest an enumeration of what the Catholics are pleased to call "the seven deadly sins." Why this distinction, thought I? Are there only seven sins? Or are only *some* sins deadly; and is the number of sins that kill ascertained by the infallible church to be just seven and no more, all other sins being venial, not mortal, according to another distinction which that church presumes to make?

They cannot mean that there are only seven sins, for *heresy* is not in this list of sins, and that I am sure they esteem a sin; neither is there any mention of *falsehood* and *deception*, which we Protestants regard as sins, even though their object should be *pious*. Besides, David says that his iniquities were more than the hairs of his head – consequently many more than seven. And who is any better off than David in this respect? Moreover, even the Catholics admit *nine* commandments. They do not leave out any but the *second*. They must therefore admit the possibility of at least nine sins.

They must mean that there are only seven sins which are mortal to the soul. But if this be the case, why is it said, "Cursed is every one that continueth not in *all things* written in the book of the law to do them?" It is admitted that there

are more than seven things written in the book of the law.
Again, why is it said that the wages of *sin* is death? This would
seem to imply that death is due to every sin, of whatever kind.
If there are only seven deadly sins, why does not the apostle
say, "The wages of these seven sins (enumerating them) is
death?" But he does not say that. He regarded all sins as deadly – every one of the multitude as mortal in its consequences.

If there are only seven sins which are deadly, then I suppose we can answer for all the rest; but *Job* says he cannot
answer him *one of a thousand*. According to Job, then, who is
a very ancient authority, there are at least a thousand sins for
which we cannot answer.

But let us hear what the seven are. They are *Pride, Covet-
ousness, Luxury* or *Lust, Anger, Gluttony, Envy, Sloth*. Well,
these are, to be sure, sins, all but one of them, *anger*, which is
not necessarily a sin any more than grief is. We are directed
to "be angry and sin not." I wonder they should have put anger
without any qualification among the seven deadly sins. It must
be because they are not familiar with the Scriptures. But granting them all to be sins, then certainly they are deadly, since all
sin is deadly. We could not therefore object, if it had been
said, in reference to them, "seven deadly sins." But *"the* seven
deadly sins" seems to imply that there are no more. We read
in the book of Proverbs of *six* things which the Lord doth hate;
yea, of seven that are an abomination to him. But there is no
implication there, that those are the only things which the Lord
hates. It is not said, *"the seven* things which the Lord doth
hate." The language which I animadvert upon implies that the
seven sins enumerated are, if not exclusively, yet peculiarly
deadly. Now that is not the case. There is nothing in those sins
to entitle them to this distinction above other sins. There is no
reason why we should be warned to avoid them more than
many others.

I am surprised that in the list of deadly sins there is no
mention of *unbelief*. Now surely that must be a deadly sin, when
"he that believeth not shall be damned – shall not see life, but
the wrath of God abideth on him." Moreover, we are told that

the Holy Ghost came primarily to reprove the world of unbe-lief – and yet there is no recognition of it among the deadly sins! It is an oversight, which no wonder they fell into, who, in making out their religion, made no use of the word of God.

I perceive that neither *heresy* nor *schism* are in the list of deadly sins. I infer, then, that to differ from the Roman church in some particulars, and even to separate from her communion, is not fatal, even she herself being judge. I thank her for the admission.

There is one sin which, in all their catalogues, the Catholics omit, and which, I think, they need to be reminded of. It is the sin of idolatry – of worshiping the creature – of paying divine honors to something else besides God. It used to be very deadly, under the Jewish dispensation. It doubtless is equally so under the Christian. They had better beware of it. They had better leave off praying to saints, and honoring the Virgin Mary above her Son, lest perchance they fall into deadly sin.

CHAPTER ELEVEN
A Religion Without the Holy Spirit

A gentleman of intelligence, who was born of Catholic parents, and educated in the Catholic church, but left it recently for Protestantism (for some do leave the Catholic for the Protestant church – the conversions are not all *to* Romanism – but we, Protestants, don't make such a noise about it when we receive a convert; and I suppose the reason is, that it is really no wonder that a Catholic should become a Protestant – the only wonder is, that any should remain Catholics) – this gentleman said to his brother, who is still a Catholic, "Why, brother, as long as I was a Catholic, I never knew that there was a Holy Spirit."

And what do you think was the brother's reply? "Well, I don't know that there is one now!"

The narration of what passed between these two men struck me with great force. A religion without a Holy Spirit! and this the religion, according to the computation of Bishop England, of *two hundred millions* of mankind! It made me sorry. My religion, thought I, would be very imperfect without a Holy Spirit. I want a Sanctifier, as well as a Surety. I want one to act internally *upon* me, as well as one to act externally *for* me. What should I do with my *title* to heaven, without a *fitness* for it? As a sinner, I am equally destitute of both. There can be no heaven without holiness. And whence has any man holiness but from the Holy Spirit? And is it likely he will act where he is not acknowledged? If priests can pardon, as they say, yet can they purify?

Here were two men, educated in the Catholic religion, and attending weekly the Catholic church, and yet never having heard of the Holy Spirit! They had heard often enough of the Virgin Mary, and of this saint, and that saint, but never a word of the Holy Spirit, the Divine Sanctifier! But was it not their own fault? Is not the doctrine of the Trinity a part of the Catholic faith? It is – but that may be, and yet the priests never instruct the people in the character and office of the Holy Spirit, and in the necessity of his operations.

But had these men never been present at a baptism, when *water*, according to Christ's direction, with *oil, spittle,* &c., as the church directs, is applied to the body, and the name of each person of the Trinity is mentioned? Yes, but, poor men, they had never studied *Latin.* How should they know what *Spiritus Sanctus* means, when they hear it? Why should all the world be presumed to understand *Latin?* Oh, why should the worship of the living God be conducted in a *dead* language? But this is by the way.

These men knew not that there was a Holy Spirit. Why did they not know it? I will tell you. Because so little is said of the Holy Spirit among the Catholics – there is so little need of any such agent, according to their system! They do not believe in the necessity of a change of heart. Why should there be a Holy Spirit? The priest does not want any such help to prepare a soul for heaven. *The Catholic system is complete without a Holy Spirit.* Therefore nothing is said of him in the pulpit, and in the confession-box; and the sinner is not directed to seek his influences, or to rely on his aid. If I misrepresent, let it be shown, and I will retract. But if I am correct in the statement I make, look at it. Protestant, look at it... a religion without a Holy Spirit! Catholic, look at it, and obey the voice from heaven which says, "Come out of her my people, that ye be not partakers of her sins, and that ye receive not of her plagues."

This is one of her *capital* crimes. She does not speak *against* the Holy Ghost. No she is silent about him!

CHAPTER TWELVE
Infallibility

Everybody knows that the Church of Rome lays claim to infallibility. She contends that there is no mistake about her; that she cannot err. Now this very modest claim of our sister of Rome (for in the matter of churches I reject the relation of mother and daughter) I am constrained to question, and that for such reasons as the following:

1. She cannot herself tell us where her infallibility is to be found. She is sure that she has it somewhere about her, but for the life of her she cannot tell where. Some of her writers say that it is with the Pope. Others contend that it resides in a general council. And another opinion is that both the Pope and a council are necessary to it. Now I think they ought to settle it among themselves *who* is infallible, before they require us to believe that *anyone* is. Let them *find* infallibility and *fix* it. After that it will be time enough for us to admit its existence. But,

2. We will suppose that it is the Pope who is infallible – each successive Pope. Well, where did they get their infallibility? Why, it was transmitted from St. Peter, to be sure. Christ gave it to him, and he handed it down. But was Peter infallible? There was a day when I suspect he did not think himself infallible – when smitten to the heart by the reproving look of

his Lord, he went out and wept bitterly. There is no doubt that he made a *mistake*, when he so confidently pronounced, "Though I should die with thee, yet will I not deny thee" and let it be remembered that this was after Christ had said, "Thou art Peter, and on this rock," &c.

If Peter was infallible, I wonder he did not at once settle the difficulty of which we have an account in Acts 15. Why was the matter suffered to be debated in the presence of his infallibility? It seems that Peter on that occasion claimed no pre-eminence. Nor was any particular deference paid to him by the council. He related his *experience*, precisely as did Paul and Barnabas. *James* seems to have been *in the chair* on that occasion. He speaks much more like an infallible person than any of the rest. He says, "Wherefore my sentence is," &c. What a pity it is for the church of Rome that Peter had not said that instead of James. We should never have heard the last of it. But it was the bishop of Jerusalem, and not the bishop of Rome, who said it. It cannot be helped now. Will my Catholic brother take down his *Douay* and read that chapter?

But again, if Peter was infallible, I am surprised that Paul *"withstood him to the face, because he was to be blamed."* Gal. 2:11. That was no way to treat a Pope. But Paul had always a *spice* of the Protestant about him. And yet Peter did not resent Paul's treatment of him, for in his second Epistle he speaks of him as "our beloved brother Paul." I suppose that Peter himself did not know he was infallible. Men do not always know themselves.

Once more, if the superiority among the disciples belonged to Peter, it has struck me as strange that, when a dispute arose among them who should be the greatest, our Savior did not take Peter, instead of a little child, "and set *him* in the midst of them," and remind the others that the *supremacy* had been given to him. I think the other apostles could not have understood Christ in that declaration, "Thou art Peter," &c. as the church of Rome now understands him, otherwise the dispute about superiority could never have arisen.

Now, according to the Catholic doctrine, Peter being infallible, each successive Pope inherits his infallibility, and therefore never a man of them could err in a matter of faith – nor even the *woman* Joan (for in the long list of *Papas*, there was by accident in the ninth century one *Mama*, though this, I am aware, is denied by some) – even she retained none of the *frailty* of her sex.

It is well for the church of Rome that she does not contend that her popes are infallible in *practice*, for if she did, she would find some difficulty in reconciling that doctrine with history. It is very true that one may err in *practice* and not in *faith*. Nevertheless, when I see a man very *crooked* in practice, I cannot believe that he is always exactly *straight* in doctrine. I cannot believe that all I hear from him is good and true, when what I see in him is false and bad. Take for example such a one as Pope Alexander sixth; when he, the father of such a hopeful youth as *Cesar Borgia*, and the chief of ecclesiastics too, tells me, with a grave air and solemn tone, that it is a shocking wicked thing for an ecclesiastic to marry, I cannot help demurring somewhat to the statement of Cesar's father.

But I must proceed with my reasons.

3. If a man says one thing one day, and the next day says another thing quite contrary to it, I am of opinion that he is one of the days in error. But what has this to do with the business in hand? Have not the Popes always pronounced the same thing? Have *they* ever contradicted each other? Ask rather, whether the wind has always, ever since there was a wind, blown from the same quarter. Now here is a reason why I cannot allow infallibility to belong to either popes or councils.

4. I would ask just for information, how it was, when there were *three* contemporary Popes, each claiming infallibility. Had they it between them? or which of them had it? What was the name of the one that there was *no mistake* about? How were the common people to ascertain the infallible one? for you know their salvation depended on their being in communion with the true Bishop of Rome, the rightful successor of St. Peter.

5. The more common opinion among the Catholics is, I be-

lieve, that the infallibility resides in a Pope and general council together. Each is fallible by itself, but putting the two together, they are infallible! Now I admit that in some languages two negatives are equivalent to an affirmative; but I do not believe that two fallibles ever were or will be equivalent to an infallible. It is like saying that *two wrongs make a right.*

CHAPTER THIRTEEN
The Keys

———◆◇◆———

The Catholics – by which I mean *Roman* Catholics, since, though a Protestant, I believe in the holy Catholic, that is, *universal* church, and profess to be a member of it, at the same time that I waive all pretensions to being a Roman Catholic – they make a great noise about the keys having been given to Peter; the keys of the kingdom of heaven. Well, it is true enough – they were given to him. The Bible says so, and we Protestants want no better authority than the Bible for anything. We do not require the confirmation of tradition, and the unanimous consent of the fathers. We do not want anything to *back* "thus saith the Lord." Yes, the keys were given to Peter; it is said so in Matthew 16:19. This is one of those passages of Scripture which is *not* hard to be understood, as even they of Rome acknowledge. I am glad our brethren of that communion agree with us that there is something plain in the Bible; that there is one passage, at least, in which private interpretation arrives at the same result which they reach who follow in the track of the agreeing fathers! I suppose, if we could interpret all Scripture as much to the mind of the Catholics as we do this, they would let us alone about private interpretation.

Well, Peter has got the keys. What then? What are keys for? To unlock and open is one of the purposes served by keys.

It was for this purpose, I suppose, that Peter received them: and for this purpose we find him using them. He opened the kingdom of heaven, that is, the Gospel Church, or Christian dispensation, as the phrase "kingdom of heaven" often signifies. He opened it to both Jews and Gentiles: he preached the first sermon, and was the instrument of making the first converts among each. With one key he opened the kingdom of heaven to the Jews, and with the other to the Gentiles. This was a distinction conferred on Peter, it is true: but it was necessary that someone of the twelve should *begin* the business of preaching the Gospel. The whole twelve could not turn the keys and open the door. The power of *binding* and *loosing*, which was conferred on Peter when the keys were given him, was not confined to him, but, as Matthew testifies in the next chapter but one, was extended to all the disciples.

Well, Peter opened the kingdom of heaven; and what became of the keys then? Why, there being no further use for them, they were laid aside. I don't know what has become of them, for my part. When a key has opened a door which is not to be shut again, there being no more use for the key, it does not matter much what becomes of it. Hence, in the history of the Acts of the Apostles, we hear no more about the keys; and Peter, in his Epistles, says never a word about them. He wrote his second Epistle to put Christians in remembrance, but I don't find him reminding them of the keys. The truth is, having used them for the purpose for which they were given him, he had after that no more concern about them.

But many fancy that Peter kept these keys all his life and then transmitted them to another, and he to a third and so from hand to hand they have come along down, till *what's his name* at Rome has them now – the Pope. And they say these keys signify the authority given to the church, and especially to the Popes. But I find no Bible warrant for this assertion. Christ does not say that he gave the keys to Peter to give to somebody else, and Peter does not say that he gave them to anybody else, and nobody since Peter has been able to produce the keys. This settles the matter in my mind. I want to know where the keys are.

But some suppose that Peter took them to heaven with him, and that he stands with them at the gate of heaven, as porter, to admit and keep out whom he will. But this notion does not tally very well with certain passages of Scripture. Christ tells his disciples that he goes to prepare a place for them, and that he will come again and receive them unto himself: John, 14:3. *He* will do it. He will not trust the business to Peter. "He that hath the key of David, he that openeth and no man shutteth, and shutteth, and no man openeth," is not Peter, but Christ. Rev. 3:7.

But the Catholics will have it that Peter is the one; and he, having the keys, they think that they will all be admitted, while never a soul of us, poor Protestants, will. They may be mistaken, however. I do not know what right they have to put in an exclusive claim to Peter. I see no resemblance between Peter and a Roman Catholic – none in the world. I never care to see a truer and better Protestant than I take him to be. But if he does stand at the gate of heaven with such authority as the Catholics ascribe to him, yet I suppose he will not deny that he wrote the Epistles called his. Well, then, if he shall hesitate to admit Protestants, we shall only have to remind him of his Epistles. He does not say anything in them about his being *Pope*. No, he says, "The elders which are among you I exhort, who am also an elder." Not a word says he about the Mass, or the Seven Sacraments, or Transubstantiation. Let the reader turn to his Epistles, and see just what he does say; I think he will not find anything in those Epistles to frighten Protestants.

But there is still another supposition, viz. that Peter is not perpetual porter of heaven; but each Pope, as he dies, succeeds to that office – one relieving another. I do not know how it is, but I judge, if all the Popes have been in their day porters of paradise, many of them must have tended *outside*. They have not been universally the best of men, I think history informs us. But I will not mention any names.

One thing more. In Catholic pictures and prints (for that very *spiritual* religion abounds with these) you will see the keys of which we have been speaking represented as made to suit all the complicated modern wards, as if fresh from some manufactory at Birmingham or Sheffield! I do not suppose the keys Peter received answered exactly to this ingenious representation of them.

CHAPTER FOURTEEN
The Head of the Church

The church is represented in the Scriptures as a *body*. Of course, therefore, it must have a *head;* and that same blessed book tells us who the head is. And who, think you, is the head of the church? Who but *Christ* himself? Who else is fit to be its head – its source of influence and government? I will produce the passages of Scripture in proof of Christ's headship presently.

But the Catholics say that the Pope is the head of the church. Ah, is he? Where is the proof that he is? Now there is nothing which irritates a Catholic so soon as to ask him for *proof.* "Proof, indeed!" he says. "Do you ask proof of an infallible church? What is the use of infallibility, if we must prove everything? These are truly most degenerate days. The time was when nobody demanded proof; but now every little sprig of a Protestant must have *reasons* to support assertions. He calls for proof. And he must have it from the Bible. He will not believe anything in religion unless some text can be cited in support of it. Things have come to a pretty pass indeed." It is even so. We plead guilty to the charge. For everything alleged to be a doctrine of Christianity, we confess we do require some proof out of the writings of some evangelist or apostle. And since our Catholic brethren will not gratify us by adducing the scriptural warrant for believing the Pope or Bishop of Rome to be the head of the church, we will do them the favor of consulting the Scriptures for them. Well, we begin with Genesis, and we go through to Revelation, searching all the way for some proof that the Pope is the head of the church. But so far are we from finding any evidence that he is the head of the church, that we find not a particle of proof that he is *that* or anything. We find no account of any such character as a Pope – not a word about him. The subject of the proposition, that is, the Pope, does not seem to be known to that book at all. I really do not wonder that it frets a Catholic when we send him to the Bible for proof that the Pope is the head of the church.

But though we discover nothing in the Bible about a Pope, yet we find much about the head of the church. In Ephesians 1:22-23, Christ is said to be "the head over all things to the church, which is *his* body." Now, if the church is his body, surely he must be the head of it, as well as head over all things to it. Will anyone say that the Pope of Rome is the head of *Christ's* body? That is shocking. And yet the Catholics are told that they *must* believe it; and seeing they cannot help it, they do somehow or other contrive to believe it. In Eph. 5:23, it is explicitly declared that "Christ is the head of the church." The same is repeated in Col. 1:18: "He [Christ] is the head of the body, the church."

Our brethren of the Catholic church have long been in the habit of asking where our religion was before the Reformation. They may see where one doctrine of it was fifteen hundred years before the Reformation. One would suppose, from the way they talk, that they supposed the Bible was written a considerable time after the Reformation, and that it was then got up to support the Protestant heresy! I might ask them, but that they do not like to be asked questions, lest they should not be able to answer them, where their doctrine of the Pope's headship of the church was when the New Testament was written – i.e., some seventeen hundred and fifty or eighteen hundred years ago. But I will withdraw the question. It may seem unkind to press it.

Now, since the Bible says that Christ is the head of the church, if the Pope also is, there must be *two* heads of the church. But there is only *one* body. Why should there be two heads? Is the church a monster? Besides, if there had been another head, Christ would have been spoken of in the Scriptures as one of the heads of the church, or as *a* head of the church. But he is called *the* head of the church. The article is definite, denoting only one. There is not a syllable in the Bible about another head. Indeed the language of the Bible does not admit of there being another. Yet the Catholics say there is another; and it is their Pope. "Christ being absent," they say, "it is necessary there should be a visible human head to represent him on earth." Now the Pope, they say, is this *visible* head of the church – the head that you can *see*. But is their assumption correct, that Christ is absent? Is he absent? Hear: "Lo, I am with you alway, even unto the end of the world." "Where two or three are gathered together in my name, there am I in the midst of them." Was he absent from Paul? He says: "I can do all things through Christ which strengtheneth me." A *visible* head! What do we want of a visible head? Of what use to us – the part of the body here – is a head a way off at Rome? It is no better than a *caput mortuum* to us.

But what if we admit the possibility of a visible human head of the church, who made the Pope that head? Did he inherit this also from St. Peter? Was Peter head of the church? He, more modest than his pretended successors, does not anywhere claim that title. I know the Catholics hold him to be the *rock* – the *foundation* of the church; but I really did not know that they regarded him, whom, however they exalt, they still consider but as a mere man, as capable of being *head* of the church too. It is not too much to speak of Christ as both the foundation and head of the church, but to speak of Peter, *poor* Peter, as we are accustomed to call him when we think of the scene of the denial, as both foundation and head of the church, is really carrying the matter rather far. How little Peter thought he was *both*, when "he went out and wept bitterly"! How little he knew of himself!

The Pope the head of the church!! Then the church is the Pope's body!! Alas for the church!

CHAPTER FIFTEEN
The Power to Forgive Sins

Seculum modestum I rather suppose will not be the designation by which the 19th century will be distinguished in history from her sister centuries. I know not whether any age has been more remarkable for cases of unfounded *pretension* than the present. The case, however, of which I am to take notice, did not originate in the 19th century. It has existed many hundred years. I do not wonder at its surviving the dark ages, but that it should have lived so far into the luminous 19th does somewhat surprise me. The pretension to which I allude is that made by the Catholic priesthood. What do you think it is which they *pretend* they can do? *Forgive sins*. They *pretend* that they have power over sins, to remit or retain them. They *claim* that the prerogative of pardon is lodged with them. And that is the reason why they receive confessions. Confession to a priest would be a farce, if it was not thought that he could forgive.

The first thing that strikes me is the contrariety of this notion to common sense. The idea of being pardoned by any other than the being offended, seems absurd. What! a fellow-sinner of a priest pardon sins against God! It is as if of *two* debtors, one should play the creditor and forgive the other his debt, without any consultation with the real creditor. That would be a strange way of getting rid of debts. I always thought he to whom the debt is due ought to have a *say* in the matter of remitting it. If I had disposed of a debt in that manner I should always be afraid that it would some day or other be exacted that the real creditor would appear and make his demand. Then it would be a poor *come off* for me to say that my fellow-debtor forgave me the debt. I will tell you what I expect. I expect that a great deal which the priests forgive will be exacted notwithstanding. Catholics talk of going to the priest and getting their *old scores wiped off*, just as if it were but a *slate and pencil* memorandum, which anyone can rub out. The sin of man is not thus recorded. It is "written with a pen of iron, and with the point of a diamond." It is not so easily obliterated.

But is there not Scripture in support of the priests' claim? See John 20:23. Does not Christ say to his disciples: "Whosoever sins ye remit, they are remitted unto them; and whosoever sins ye retain, they are retained?" Yes, he says that *to his disciples – the apostles*. But pray, what right have the priests to found a claim of theirs on a grant made to the apostles? They do indeed *come after* the apostles, but they are their *successors* in no other sense. I should like to know how the priests *prove* that they inherit the apostolical power of remitting sins. But I forget that they scorn a resort to *proof*.

The power communicated in that grant to the apostles was merely *ministerial* and *declarative*. It was no less true after than before that grant was made, that none can forgive sins but God only. That the power was *declarative* merely, that is, that the apostles were empowered to remit and retain sins only as they were authorized and enabled to make a correct statement to mankind of the way and means of salvation, to express the conditions of pardon and condemnation, and to propose the terms of life and death, is clear to me from the fact that the conferring of it was immediately preceded by the Savior's breathing on them, and saying, "Receive ye the Holy Ghost." Now this communication of the Spirit qualified them for the *declarative* remission and retention of sins. They were thereby inspired to pronounce on what grounds sins are remitted and retained by God.

This was the power over sins granted to the apostles, and I shall show presently that this *declarative* power is all they pretend ever to have exercised. Now, the priests have no right to claim even this power, except in that subordinate sense in which it is possessed by all who are authorized to preach the Gospel. Did Christ ever breathe on them, and say to them, "Receive ye the Holy Ghost," that they should claim equality with the apostles? The effect of the *inspiration* is not so manifest in the case of the priests as it was in the case of the apostles, if I may be permitted to express an opinion.

But the priests claim far more than ever entered the thoughts of the apostles. They are not satisfied with the ministerial and declarative power over sins They claim a *magisterial* and *authoritative* power to remit and retain them. Consequently they call sinners to come and confess their sins to them. Did Peter and the other apostles, the very men to whom Christ said, "whosoever sins ye remit," &c. ever do such a thing? You read in the Acts of the Apostles of *synagogues* and *proseuches*. or places of prayer, but do you find anything about *confession-boxes* there? Does there seem to have been anything *auricular* in the transactions of the day of Pentecost?

There is the case of Simon Magus that strikes me as in point. If Peter and John had had the power of forgiving sin, could they not have exercised it in favor of Simon? But we find Peter addressing him just as any Protestant minister would have done: "Repent therefore of this thy wickedness, and pray God, if perhaps the thought of thine heart may be forgiven thee." How differently the Roman priest would have done! He would have said, "Well, Simon, and what have you to say for yourself? Ah, that is very bad, very bad. But if you are sorry, Simon, I forgive you. Only I cannot let you off without doing some penance. You must say so many *paternosters*, and you must not eat meat for so many days." This is the way in which the boasted successors of Peter manage these matters. But, they will say, Simon was not penitent, otherwise perhaps Peter would have pardoned him. But I wonder if pardon would have waited for Peter's action in the matter, if there had been penitence in the heart of the sorceror. I suspect not. I suspect the gracious Lord, when he sees contrition in any soul, does not withhold pardon till a priest or even an apostle shall intervene and act in the matter. And when the good angels have ascertained that a sinner has repented, I rather suppose they do not suspend their rejoicing until he has gone to confession, and has got absolution from the priest.

What a glorious book the Bible is! I wish the authorities of the Catholic church would condescend to strike it off the list of *prohibited* books, and *allow* the Lord to speak to his creatures. I wish they would let their people, the many thousands that on the Sabbath crowd their chapels and cathedrals, read, or hear what Jehovah says to "every one" in that wonderful chapter, the 55th of Isaiah. It is indeed a wonderful chapter. But the Catholics don't know anything about it. No; and they have never heard of that precious and glorious verse, the 18th of the 1st chapter of Isaiah, in which thus saith the Lord to the sinner, "Come now, and let us" (you and I, sinner!) "reason together." And then follows the reasoning, "though your sins be as scarlet, they shall be as white as snow; though they be red like crimson, they shall be as wool." Ask the awakened sinner, or the recently pardoned, what he would take for that passage. He esteems it above all price; and to the Christian it becomes every day more and more a theme of wonder and delight. But the Catholics don't know that the Lord has ever made any such kind and condescending proposal to his creatures. They never hear of the call of God to come and reason with him. The only "come" they hear is the priest's call. I pity them.

But it is no wonder that the priests treat the people as they do, for if they allowed them to know what the Lord says to them, they would be very apt to go directly to God in Christ, and leave the priest out of the question. And then where would be the importance of the priest? and his *emolument*, where?

CHAPTER SIXTEEN
A Catholic Book Reviewed

I happened to lay my hand the other day on a little book entitled, *The Christian's Guide to Heaven: A Manual For Catholics*, to which was appended some hymns. The book was published in Baltimore by a respectable Catholic bookseller, and under the sanction of the Archbishop. Well, said I to myself, this is good authority. I will look into this book. I know what Protestants say of Catholics. I will see now what Catholics say of themselves. Men cannot complain when we take their own account of themselves; and I like the way of judging people out of their own mouths, because it shuts their mouths so far as reply is concerned. I resolved that I would compare the statements and doctrines of this book professing to be a guide to heaven, with the statements and doctrines of that bigger book which is the Protestant's guide to heaven. You will know that I mean the Bible. That is our manual – that is the guide we consult and follow. However, if a book agrees with the Bible, that is enough.

So I began to read; and one of the first things that I came to was, "Conditions of Plenary Indulgences." Indulgences! thought I. What does a Christian want of indulgences? He is apt enough to indulge himself. And how are indulgences to help him to heaven? I should rather pronounce self-denial the road. Indulgences not *partial*, but *plenary!* I should think plenary indulgence on any condition was enough to ruin one. If by indulgence the Catholics mean pardon, they have chosen an unfortunate way to express it. Why not say *full pardon*, instead of plenary indulgence? But I suppose pardon expresses what God exercises, and indulgence what the church grants. I should like to know, however, what right the church has to grant anything of the kind.

Well, the conditions enumerated were four. I took note only of the first, which was in these words: "To confess their sins with a sincere repentance to a priest approved by the bishop." This begins very well, and goes on well for a time. Confession of sin, with sincere repentance, *is* truly a condition of pardon. "If we confess our sins, he is faithful and just to forgive us our sins." But what a pity the condition did not stop there, or if anything was added in regard to the object of the confession, that it did not designate God as the Being to whom the sins should be confessed. The sins are all *done* against him, and why should they not be *told* to him? I cannot get rid of the notion that we ought to confess our sins to God, the Being whom we have offended by them. But no, says this guide to heaven, the confession must be made to a priest; it is good for nothing without it. If the publican, of whom we read, had lived now, it would have been quite irregular, according to the Catholic notion, that he should have gone down to his house justified, when he confessed only to God. And the penitent must take care what sort of a priest it is to whom he confesses, else he might as well remain impenitent. It must be a priest *approved by the bishop*. Well, now, this is a queer arrangement, that our pardon should be suspended on such a condition – that angels, in other words, must wait before they express any joy that a sinner has repented, until he has gone and told his sins to a priest approved by a bishop! Who suspended it there, I wonder? Not Isaiah. Read his 55th chapter. Nor Peter, nor Solomon, nor John, nor Paul. Read them and see. There is not a word in the Bible about confessing to a priest. So I found that the two guides did not agree in this matter. The Catholic manual said the confession must be to a priest; but the holy Scriptures insist on no such thing, but direct that the confession be made to God.

This thought occurred to me: What if a sinner confess his sins with a sincere repentance, though not to a priest, what is to be done with his soul? Must pardon be denied him, and he be consigned to perdition, because, though he confessed penitently, yet he did it not to a priest? Really this is making rather too much of the priest. It is making too important a character of him altogether. I do not believe that our salvation is so dependent on the deference we pay the priest.

Before the conditions, on one of which I have been remarking, are mentioned, there is this general statement: "Plenary indulgences granted to the faithful through out these states, *at the following times;*" and then follows a specification of nine different seasons when plenary indulgences may be had. I did not know before that pardons were confined to any set times; I always supposed that they might be had summer and winter, night and day, and at any hour of either – in short, whenever a penitent heart breathes its desire to God. My mistake must have arisen from the fact that I have been in the habit of consulting the Bible on these matters. I never saw the *Christian's Guide to Heaven* before in my life. I have always used the Bible as a guide, for want of a better.

Now that I am on the subject of confession, I may as well make another reference to the manual. There is an article or chapter headed "The Confiteor." In it the person wishing to be guided to heaven makes this confession, from which it will appear that Catholics do not confine their confessions to the priest, but extend them to many other beings: "I confess to Almighty God, to blessed Mary, ever virgin, to blessed Michael the archangel, to blessed John the Baptist, to the holy apostles Peter and Paul, and to all the saints, that I have sinned." Now, I do not see the use of naming so many. The confession, I think, should have stopped with the first mentioned – Almighty God.

What have the rest to do with it? How is it any of their business? The person has not sinned against them. Surely every sinner may say to God, "Against thee, thee *only* have I sinned," since David could. Besides, this coupling of these creatures with the Creator, as worthy equally with himself to receive our confessions of sin, savors strongly of idolatry. Confession is made to him on the same principle that prayer is. Each is an act of worship – one of those things which should be confined exclusively to God. I wonder the Catholics will not be satisfied with one great and glorious object of worship, God, the Father, Son, and Spirit. Why will they in their devotions associate creatures with the Creator? The book I am reviewing contains numerous and very offensive examples of it. I shall continue the review in my next.

CHAPTER SEVENTEEN
Review of the Catholic Book Continued

The next thing that struck me as worthy of notice in the perusal of the book was this – that the devout Catholic is represented as making the following solemn declaration concerning the Holy Scriptures: "Neither will I ever take and interpret them otherwise than according to the unanimous consent of the fathers." I smiled when I read this, and I thought within myself, if that is his determination, he will not be likely ever to take them at all. What an intention this, which the Catholic expresses – never to attach any meaning to a passage which he may read in the Bible, until he has first ascertained *whether* certain ancient persons called the fathers all agreed in any interpretation of it, and if so, what that interpretation is! What should give such authority and weight to the interpretation of the fathers? Why cannot we ascertain what the Bible means as well as they could? What helps had they which we have not? and why require that they be unanimous? What a roundabout method this is of finding out what a book means! First, the reader has got to ascertain who are entitled to be called *fathers*. He must make out a list of them all. If one is overlooked, it vitiates the interpretation, though all the rest should agree in it. But supposing him to have got a catalogue of the whole number from Barnabas to Bernard, the *next* step in the process is to ascertain how they all interpreted the Bible. For this purpose he must pore over their works. But some of them left no works behind them. How shall he ever find out what they thought of this and that passage of Scripture? And yet he must somehow or other ascertain their opinions, else how can he compare them with the opinions of the other fathers, and discover their agreement with them? For you will remember the consent must be *unanimous*. Others of the fathers left works behind them, but they have not come down to us. How shall the reader of the Bible know what those lost works contained? Yet he must know what they thought, else how can he be sure that they thought in accordance with the views of those fathers whose works are preserved to us? I cannot see how this difficulty is to be got over, for my part. It is altogether beyond me. But supposing it to be surmounted, there remains the task of comparing the opinions of all these Greek and Latin fathers, to the number of a hundred or two, one with another, to see if they all agree; for the consent, you know, must be unanimous. Those parts of Scripture in the interpretation of which they did not agree, are to go for nothing. Indeed, if ninety-nine should be found to accord in a particular interpretation, it must be rejected if the hundredth father had a different opinion of its meaning. I cannot help thinking that it is the better, as certainly it is the shorter and easier method, just for everyone to take up and "search the Scriptures," and "if any lack wisdom, let him ask of God, that giveth to all men liberally."

As the case is, I do not wonder that the Catholics do not read the Bible. They have not come to that yet. They are still among the fathers, searching out and comparing their opinions, so as to know how to *take* the Bible. By and by, if they live long enough, when they have ascertained what the fathers agreed on, they may go to reading the Scriptures.

It seems odd that one cannot, without mortal sin, attach a meaning to such a passage as John 3:16, "God so loved the world, that he gave his only begotten Son, that whosoever believeth in him should not perish, but have everlasting life," until he has first ascertained what Cyprian, Jerome, Hilary, both the Gregorys, and indeed all the fathers thought of it, and whether they agreed in their interpretation of it. How anyone can read it without understanding it in spite of himself, I cannot see. Ah, but they say the Scriptures are so obscure. And are the fathers so very *clear?* Why cannot we understand the Greek of John and Paul, as well as that of Chrysostom?

The thing which next attracted my observation in the book was the following: "In the Mass there is offered to God a true, proper, and propitiatory sacrifice for the living and the dead." The Mass! and what is that? The *Bible* could not tell me. So I had to resort to the *dictionary.* It is the name which the Catholics give to the sacrament of the Lord's supper; or rather to the *half* of it; for you know they divide it, and giving the bread to the people, do with the wine I cannot tell what. They say that it is *perfect in one kind,* and anathematize all who say it is not. Their curse is on me now while I am writing. Nevertheless I must ask, if it was perfect in one kind, why did Christ institute it in both kinds? Why did he not stop with the bread, reserving the cup? Was it to make the sacrament more than perfect? But this is *reasoning.* I forget myself. The Catholics don't hold to reasoning.

An idea occurs to me here which I beg leave to express. If the sacrament is perfect in *either* kind, why do not the priests sometimes give the people the cup? Why do they always give them the bread? And why originally did they withhold the cup rather than the bread? Some persons may imagine a reason, but I will content myself with asking the question.

But to proceed. They say that "in the Mass *there is offered to God,"* &c. Why, what do they mean? There is nothing offered to God. What is offered is to men. Christ says, offering to his disciples the bread, "take, eat," and reaching out the cup, he says, "drink ye *all* of it." There is something offered to men in this sacrament, even the precious memorials of the Saviors propitiatory death; but everyone who reads the account, sees that there is nothing offered to God. Yet the Catholics, leaning on tradition, say there is in it "a true, proper and propitiatory sacrifice" offered to God. A sacrifice included in the sacrament! How is that? And a *propitiatory* sacrifice too! I always supposed that propitiatory sacrifices ceased with the offering up of the Great Sacrifice – when the Lamb of God bled and died. Do we not read, that "by one offering he hath perfected for ever them that are sanctified," "now *once* in the end of the world hath he appeared to put away sin by the sacrifice of himself"? "Christ was *once* offered to bear the sins of many" – and it is said of his blood that it "cleanseth from all sin." I don't know what we want after this, of those unbloody sacrifices which the Catholics talk of as offered continually in the service of the Mass. What is the use of them, if they are *unbloody,* as they say, since "without shedding of blood is no remission?"

According to the Catholics, it was premature in Christ to say on the cross, "It is finished." They deny that it is finished. They say *it is going on* still – that Christ is offered whenever Mass is said. *Once* Christ was offered, the Bible says; but the Roman church affirms that he is offered many times daily, whenever and wherever Mass is said!

I do really wonder that this religion has lasted so long in the world. How the human mind can entertain it for a day, I do not know. See how at every step it conflicts with reason. See in how many points it does violence to common sense. See, in this case, how boldly it contradicts the dying declaration of the Savior. It is a religion unknown to the Bible – and yet still in existence, aye, and they say, *making progress,* and that even in this home of freedom! If it be so, which I question, I blush that I am an American, and am almost ashamed that I am a man.

CHAPTER EIGHTEEN
The Pope an Idolater

It may seem a very uncharitable title I give this article. What, some will say, charge the Pope with being an idolater! What do you mean? I mean just what I say, that this boasted head of the church, and self-styled vicar of Christ, residing at Rome, ascribes divine attributes, and pays divine honors to a creature, even to a human being, a partaker in our mortality and sin! and if that is not idolatry, I don't know what idolatry is. If that is not idolatry, the worship of the golden calf was not – the worship of the host of heaven was not – the worship of the gods of Hindooism is not. What truer definition of idolatry can be given than that it is an ascribing of divine attributes, and a paying of divine honors to a creature? It does not matter what the creature is, whether it be the angel nearest the throne of God, or an onion that grows in the garden, such as they of Egypt once worshiped. It is its being a created thing – it is its being *not God,* that makes the service done it idolatry.

But can I make good this charge against the successor of St. Peter, as they call him? If I cannot, I sin not merely against charity, but against truth. But I can establish it. Nor will I derive the proof from the Pope's enemies; nor will I look for it in the histories of the Papacy. The Pope himself shall supply me with the proof. Out of his own mouth will I judge him. If

his own words do not convict him of idolatry, believe it not.
But if they do, away with the objection that it is an offence
against charity to speak of such a thing as the Pope's being an
idolater. My charity "rejoiceth in the truth." The charge can
be uncharitable only by being untrue. It is too late in the day,
I trust, for idolatry to find an apologist. But to the proof. Perhaps you suppose it is some obscure Pope of the night of
times the dark ages, that I am going to prove an idolater. No,
it is a Pope of the nineteenth century – the present reigning
Pope, Gregory XVI. He is the idolater; and here are his own
"words in proof of it. They are a part of the circular, or encyclical letter, sent forth by him on entering on his office, and
addressed to all Patriarchs, Primates, Archbishops, and Bishops. The letter may be found in the *Laity's Directory*, 1833,
and has been extensively published without any of its statements being contradicted. In it the Pope calls upon all the
clergy to implore "that she [the Virgin Mary] who has been,
through every great calamity, our Patroness and Protectress,
may watch over us writing to you, and lead our mind by her
heavenly influence, to those counsels which may prove most
salutary to Christ's flock!" Is comment necessary? Observe,
he recognizes *not God* as having been their defence, but *her*
as having been their protectress in past calamities, and directs
the clergy to pray to her to continue her watch over them! As
contrast is one of the principles on which ideas are associated,
I was reminded in reading this, of the 121st Psalm, in which
the writer speaks of the one "that keepeth Israel." It is not *she,*
according to the Psalmist, but *he,* the Lord which made
heaven and earth, that keepeth Israel. But, according to the
Pope, it is the Virgin Mary that keeps Israel; and he speaks of
her as exerting a heavenly influence on the mind. I always
thought it was the exclusive prerogative of Jehovah to have
access to the mind, and to exert an immediate influence on it;
and I cannot but think now that the Pope must err in this matter, though he speaks *ex cathedra*. I cannot believe he was
exactly *infallible* when he wrote that letter.

But you have not heard the worst of it yet. In the same letter he says: "But that all may have a successful and happy issue, *let us raise our eyes* to the most blessed Virgin Mary, *who alone destroys heresies, who is our greatest hope,* yea, the ENTIRE GROUND OF OUR HOPE!" The underscoring is mine, but the words are the Pope's. Now, just look at this. Did you ever hear anything like it? Observe what Mary is said to be and to do; and what the clergy are exhorted to do. The Pope's religion cannot be the *oldest*, as they pretend. It is not the religion of the *Psalms*. In the 121st Psalm the writer says: *"I* will lift up mine eyes unto the hills, from whence cometh my help. My help cometh from the Lord." And in the 123d, "Unto thee lift I up mine eyes, O thou that dwellest in the heavens. Behold, as the eyes of servants look unto the hand of their masters, and as the eyes of a maiden unto the hand of her mistress; so our eyes wait upon the Lord our God, until that he have mercy upon us." But the Pope says: "Let us raise our eyes to the most blessed Virgin Mary." There is the difference between the Pope and the Psalmist. Protestants in this case side with the Psalmist; and in this particular our religion is not only older than Luther, but older even than the Pope.

I would inquire of the reader whether these prayers which the Pope would have the whole church address to the Virgin Mary, are not precisely such as are proper to be addressed to God, and which others do address to him? Do they not ask of *her* just what ought to be asked of *him*, and what he alone can give? After asking such things as the Catholics are directed to ask of the Virgin Mary, what remains to be asked of God in prayer? And is not this putting a creature in the place of God? Indeed, is it not putting God quite out of the question? The eyes are raised in prayer to the Virgin, and they are lifted no higher. There they fix. Is not this idolatry? And you see he is not satisfied himself with being an idolater, but he wants the entire clergy, and of course the whole Catholic church, to join him in his idolatry!

I wish the Pope had explained how the blessed Virgin *de-*

stroys heresies. He says she does it, and she alone. I should think it rather belonged to "the Spirit of Truth" to destroy heresies, and to "guide into all truth." But no, says the Pope, the Spirit of Truth has nothing to do with it. It is all done by the blessed Virgin! She *"alone* destroys heresies."

The Catholics complain that we call their Pope *Antichrist.* But I would appeal to anyone to say if he is not Antichrist, who, overlooking Christ altogether, says of another, that *she* is "our greatest hope, yea, the entire ground of our hope?" Is not that against Christ? The Bible speaks of *him* as "our hope," 1 Tim. 1:1; yea, of him as our *only* hope; for "other foundation can no man lay than that is laid, which is Jesus Christ." 1 Cor. 3:11. "Neither is there salvation in any other." Acts 4:12. It would seem from this, that Christ is the *ground of hope.* But not so, says the Pope; the blessed Virgin is "the entire ground of our hope." By the way, I should not be surprised if that hope should disappoint its possessor. Now, is not the Pope Antichrist? Well, if he is an idolater and Antichrist, ought he to be adhered to? What sort of a body must that be, which has such a head? I think I should not like to be a *member* of it. And I must confess that I am against such a person having any more power in our free, enlightened, and happy America, than he has already. Pray let us not, after having broken the chains of political thraldom, come in bondage to idolatry. Let us not, after having extricated our persons from the power of a king, subject our *minds* to the spiritual domination of a *Pope.*

CHAPTER NINETEEN
Charles X. an Idolater

Having proved his holiness the Pope an idolater, I proceed now to prove "his most Christian majesty" *that was,* the ex-king of France, an idolater; which having done, I shall have gone a good way towards proving the whole Catholic church idolatrous, since, as you know, it is their boast that they all think alike, and that there are no such varieties of opinion among them as among us unfortunate Protestants; though, by the way, it is not so strange that they all think alike, when one thinks for all.

I proved *Gregory* an idolater out of his own mouth. I shall do the same in the case of *Charles.* On the occasion of the baptism (with *oil, spittle,* &c. – an improvement on the simple water-system of the Bible) of his young grand-son, the Duke of Bordeaux, this was his language: "Let us invoke for him the protection of the mother of God, the queen of the angels; let us implore her to watch over his days, and remove far from his cradle the misfortunes with which it has pleased Providence to afflict his relatives, and to conduct him by a less rugged path than I have had, to eternal felicity." He was anxious that the little boy should have a protector, one to watch over him, and to remove his misfortunes, and to conduct him by an easy path to eternal life. For this purpose, one not educated a Catholic would have supposed that he would apply to

the omniscient and almighty God. I do not know who can do
those things besides God. But no. "His majesty" does no more
apply to God, than did his holiness in a similar case. I suppose
it would have been heresy if he had. They would have thought
him going over to Protestantism. His Holiness and his Majesty both make application to the creature rather than to the
Creator. Charles does not say, "Let us invoke for him the protection of God," but of a woman – a woman indeed highly
favored of the Lord, and of blessed memory, but still a
woman.

He calls her, according to the custom of his church, "the
mother of God." I suppose you know that phrase is not in the
Bible. And there is a good reason for it – the idea is not as old
as the Bible. The Bible is an old book, almost as old as our
religion. Roman Catholicism is comparatively young. I will
not remark on the phrase, *mother of God,* seeing it is not in
the Bible, and since it has often been remarked upon by others. But there is another thing the ex-king says of her, on
which I will spend a word or two. He calls her "the queen of
the angels." Now we read in the Bible, of Michael, the archangel, or prince of angels, but we do not read of the angels
having a queen. We read also of a *king* in heaven, but not a
word about a queen. I don't know where he got this idea of a
queen of angels. He certainly did not get it out of the Holy
Scriptures, and yet these Scriptures, I had always supposed,
contain all that we know about the angels. I wish he would tell
us from his retirement where he got the idea, for he speaks
very positively about the angels having a queen. It is true, we
do read in one place in the Bible of a *queen of heaven,* but the
worship of her was so evidently idolatry, that I presume the
Catholics will not quote it as authorizing the title they give
and the honor they pay to the Virgin Mary. The account is
found in Jeremiah 44. If anyone will read the chapter he will
see what that prophet thought of those worshipers of the
queen of heaven. Now, if the worship of a queen of heaven by
the Jews was denounced as idolatry, and ruin came on them

in consequence of it, is not a similar worship performed by Catholics as idolatrous, and as dangerous?

But no matter what he calls her, he asks her to do what only God can do. He treats her precisely as if she were divine. Is it not so – and is not this idolatry? He ascribes divine perfections to her – omniscience, else how could she watch over the child; and omnipotence, else how could she ward off evil from him; and he speaks of her as the guide of souls to eternal life. The Psalmist considered it was the prerogative of God to do this. He says, "Thou shalt guide me with thy counsel, and afterward receive me to glory." But the ex-king looks to Mary to conduct the young duke to eternal life. What the Psalmist expects from God, the ex-king expects from Mary. Is not this putting a creature in the place of God, the Creator? Everyone must see that it is shocking idolatry, and that the man who uses such language is as truly an idolater as any devotee of Juggernaut.

I do really wonder that the Catholics continue to call their system Christianity. It is by a great misnomer it is so called. It is not the proper name for it at all. It should be called by some such name as *Marianism,* rather than Christianity. In Christianity the principal figure is Christ; but he is not the principal figure in the Catholic religion. Mary is. Therefore the religion should be called after her, Marianism, and not after Christ, Christianity. Catholics are not the disciples of Christ, but of Mary; she is their confidence and hope. Pope Gregory says *she* "is our greatest hope, yea, the entire ground of our hope." Now, I think that the religion of such people ought to be called after the one who is their greatest hope; and I have suggested a name to the Catholics, which I advise them to adopt. Let their religion be called *Marianism,* and let them leave to us the name Christianity, since Christ "is *our* hope."

Having proved his Holiness, and his most Christian Majesty, the two principal characters in the church of Rome, idolaters, I think I may as well stop here.

CHAPTER TWENTY
Idolatry Near Home

It is wonderful what a propensity there is in fallen men to idolatry. How they do love to worship the creature rather than the Creator! In a certain church, which need not be named, the blessed Virgin, though a mere woman, receives ten, perhaps a hundred times as much religious honor as does the blessed Savior, though he be "the mighty God," deserving of all homage, while she merits barely respectful remembrance. One that has much intercourse with Catholics would suppose the *mother* to be the Savior of the world, rather than the *Son*. They make her to be the principal advocate of sinners in heaven. "If any man sin, we have an advocate with the Father." Who? St. John says, *"Jesus Christ* the righteous" – the Catholics say it is *Mary!* So they differ – we Protestants side with John.

I have lately met with an idolatrous temple, that is, a church or chapel avowedly erected in honor of a creature, and dedicated to a creature. Is not that a temple of idolatry? Can there be a more accurate definition of such a place? Well, I have seen one – and I have not been a voyage to *India* neither. Some think there is no idolatry nearer than India; and when they hear of an idol-temple they immediately think of Juggernaut. But it is a mistake. I have not been out of the United

States of America, and yet I have seen a temple of idolatry. I will state the case, and let everyone judge for himself. If I am under an erroneous impression I shall be glad to be corrected. The case is this: On the Catholic chapel in *Annapolis, Maryland,* is this inscription, "IN HONOREM DEI PA RÆ VIRGINIS." It is Latin. The English of it is, "In honor of the Virgin, the Mother of God." If I have not rightly translated it, some of those who worship in Latin can correct me.

Now, what does this mean? It seems to signify that the chapel was erected, and is continued in honor of, that is, *for the worship* of the Virgin Mary. The being in whose honor a chapel is erected is worshiped in it. If not, how is it in honor of him? The inscription signifies *dedication* to the Virgin Mary. Now, the being to whom a place of religious worship is dedicated is always the object of the worship there rendered. This is universally understood. Hence we dedicate our churches to the Triune God, for him we worship in them. They are erected *in honor* of him. No one mistakes the meaning of these inscriptions. When we read on the Unitarian church in Baltimore this inscription in Greek, "To the only God," we understand that the church is consecrated to the service of the only God, and it is precisely the same as if the inscription had been in the style of that at Annapolis, *in honor* of the only God. So when Paul found at Athens an altar with this inscription, "To the unknown God," he inferred immediately that worship was intended, for he says, "whom therefore ye ignorantly worship." Suppose the inscription had been "in honor of the unknown God," would not the apostle's inference have been the same? Nothing is more clear than that the inscription on which I am remarking implies that the chapel in question is dedicated to the worship of the Virgin Mary; and she being a creature, this constitutes it a temple of idolatry, and those who worship in it idolaters!

Let no man say that the inscription implies no more than that the chapel is named after Mary. Some Protestants name their churches after saints, but the name is not given in any case *in honor* of the saint. St. Paul's in London was not built in honor of St. Paul. It is simply so denominated. But here we have a chapel *in honor* of the Virgin, and she is called *Mother of God,* apparently to justify the worship which the authors of the chapel intend her. If this were the only proof that Catholics worship the Virgin Mary, we might overlook it; but it is only one of many. No one thing is more susceptible of demonstration, less capable of denial, than that Roman Catholics render unto this creature that which is due to God alone, religious worship. See for proof, their own Rhemish Testament with the notes. *Therefore they are idolaters.* I am sorry to say it, because I am sorry there is any occasion for saying it. But the time has come to speak out. This religion is threatening America, and it should be known, it should be proclaimed in the ear of every Christian, and every patriot, that it is something worse than mere *error.* And something more to be dreaded far than *tyranny*, which also it is, and ever has been, and must be – it is IDOLATRY. It puts another, and a creature, in the place of God; or if it discards not him, it does what is as offensive to him, it associates other and inferior objects of worship with him – and this his jealousy will not suffer. Whatever this great people are to become, I do hope we shall never be a nation of idolaters – creature-worshipers. We had better be, what God forbid we ever should be, a nation of slaves. I do verily believe that the Roman Catholic religion has only to be universally adopted to make us *both*.

CHAPTER TWENTY-ONE
Praying to Saints

———◈———

This is one of the numerous points on which Catholics and Protestants differ from each other. They, the Catholics, pray to departed saints. This they acknowledge they do, nor are they at all ashamed of the practice, but endeavor to justify it. If anyone doubts that they hold to the *invocation of saints*, as they express it, let him consult the notes to their own Rhemish Testament, or look into their book of prayers, where he will read the very language in which they make their supplication to the saints.

We Protestants do *not* pray to saints, and we think we have pretty good reasons for not doing it. We will mention some of them, in the hope that they will appear to be equally good reasons why Catholics should not pray to saints.

1. We do not feel the need of saints to pray to. We have a great and good God to go unto, whose ear is ever open to our cry, and we think that is enough; we do not want any other object of prayer. Whenever we feel the need of anything, we judge it best to apply directly to our heavenly Father, especially since James, one of the saints, testifies, that "every good gift, and every perfect gift, is from above, and cometh down from the Father of lights." Others may, in their necessity, if they please, apply to the saints, but we choose to ask of the

Great Giver of all good. In doing so, we think we are much more likely to receive than if we invoke the saints.

It is true, being sinners, we need an advocate with the Father, but we do not need more than one, and him we have, as John, another saint, testifies, in Jesus Christ: "If any man sin, we have an advocate with the Father, Jesus Christ the righteous." John speaks of only one advocate, and Paul asserts that as there is but one God, so there is but one *mediator* between God and men. Yet the Catholics will have it, that there are advocates many and mediators many. The notes of the Rhemish translators on 1 Tim. 2:5, and 1 John 2:1, assert the doctrine of a plurality of mediators and advocates. The object of those notes is to show, that if any man sin, he has many advocates with the Father, and that there are more mediators than one between God and men; the very reverse of what those texts assert! I am aware that the Catholics say that saints are mediators only in a subordinate sense; but I say they are mediators in no sense. Does the Bible speak of them as mediators in *any* sense? Those words, "mediator" and "advocate," are in the Bible sacredly appropriated to Christ. There is but one, and it is he. We come to the Father by him. *To* him we come immediately. Here we need no daysman.

2. We Protestants have always regarded prayer as a part of worship, as much as praise and confession of sin. Now, our Savior says, "Thou shalt worship the Lord thy God, and him *only* shalt thou serve." We dare not, therefore, pray to any other than God. We would not like to be guilty of the idolatry of worshiping a creature.

3. If we were disposed to pray to the saints, yet we should not exactly know how to do it. Were we to pray to them generally, without singling any out by name, it would be a kind of praying at random; and we strongly suspect that our requests would not be attended to, for it may be among saints in heaven, as it is among their less perfect brethren on earth, that what is made everybody's business comes to be regarded as nobody's. If, on the other hand, we apply to specific saints,

and invoke them by name, this supposes that we know just who the saints are. It implies either that we could see into their hearts while they lived, or that we can see into heaven now – both which far outreach our power. We might make some sad mistake in praying to deceased men who have passed for saints. It is easy enough to ascertain who the church regards as saints, but the canonized may not exactly correspond to the sanctified. But, supposing this difficulty removed, and that we know certain individuals, who, having once lived on earth, are now in heaven: the next thing is, to make them hear us, for there is manifestly no use in preferring requests to those who cannot hear them. How is this to be done? The saints are in heaven – the suppliant sinner is on earth, and the distance between them is great. Saints in heaven are not within call of sinners on earth. Where is the proof of it? If I say, "Peter, pray for me," how is he to know I say it? Peter is not omnipresent. Do they say that God communicates to him the fact; but where is the proof of that? Besides, what does it amount to? God, according to this theory, informs Peter that a certain sinner on earth wants him, Peter, to ask him, the Lord, to grant him something. This is a roundabout method of getting at the thing. The man had better, a great deal, not trouble Peter, but say at once, "God be merciful to me a sinner."

But the Catholics ask with an air of triumph, if we do not request living saints to pray for us. We do, for we have in-spired authority for that. But that is not praying to them. There is a wide difference between praying to a saint in heaven, and asking a fellow-traveler to Zion on earth to pray to God for us. Everyone must see that. When a Christian asks his minister or his Christian friend to beseech God for him, he does not con-sider that he is praying to him or invoking him. Besides, we never ask one to pray for us, unless we know he is within hear-ing. We should think it very silly to do so. We must have proof of his presence before we think of making any request of him. Yet the Catholics are continually making requests of creatures, of whose presence with them they have not a particle of proof, and who, being creatures, it is certain cannot be present with *all* that call upon them. How many individuals are every day, at the same hour, calling on the blessed Virgin for assistance! It is all folly, unless she be omnipresent – a goddess, which the Bible certainly does not represent her as being. She occupies but one small spot in the universe of God, and it is probably a great way off. She cannot hear, even if she could help. Do you suppose that her calm repose in heaven is suffered to be disturbed by the ten thousand confused voices that cry to her without ceasing from earth? Never.

In looking over the Bible, the book which contains the religion of Protestants, and which, being older than the Roman Catholic religion, proves the seniority of Protestantism over Popery, I find no account of praying to saints. I do not read of Joshua praying to Moses; or of Elisha invoking Elijah. No, there is not a word of what constitutes so much of the devotion of the Catholic in either Testament. We do not find anything in the Acts or Epistles about praying to the beloved Virgin, whom they call *our Lady,* in allusion to the phrase *our Lord.* Those writers say nothing about the *mother.* It is all about the Son. What heretics Luke and the rest of them were! How worthy of being excommunicated! Catholic books are full of the blessed Virgin. The Bible is all about Christ. There is the difference.

But I forgot. The New Testament does record one instance of prayer to a departed saint. The record is in Luke 16. The saint prayed to was Abraham. The supplicant was a rich man in hell, and he made two requests. Here is the Catholic's authority for this doctrine of praying to deceased saints, so far as he gets it out of the Bible. Let him make the most of it. When, however, he takes into consideration that it was offered from hell, and by a man who lived and died in ignorance and neglect of religion, and that it proved totally unavailing, I suspect he will make no more out of it.

CHAPTER TWENTY-TWO
Specimens of Catholic Idolatry

I take them from the Catholic book which I have been reviewing, *The Christian's Guide to Heaven*. I did not know, before I read this book, that idolatry was the road to heaven. It did not use to be under the Jewish dispensation. These specimens of Catholic idolatry I think the reader will pronounce, with me, quite up to the average of Pagan idolatry.

Here is one. "We fly to thy patronage, O holy mother of God; despise not our petitions in our necessities, but deliver us from all dangers." That is the manner in which devout Catholics in the United States are directed to pray. They fly to Mary, but "God is *our* refuge." There is the difference. They look to her to deliver them from all dangers. I don't know how she can deliver them from all dangers. I think they had better ascertain the powers of the Virgin Mary, before they place such unbounded reliance on her. I should be a very fearful creature, had I none to fly to from danger but her. "What time I am afraid, I will trust in *thee*" (the Lord). So says the Psalmist, and it is my purpose too.

The next specimen is entitled, "The Salve Regina," and thus it runs: "Hail! holy queen, mother of mercy, our life, our sweetness, and our hope. To thee we cry, poor banished sons of Eve; to thee we send up our sighs, mournings and weeping in this valley of tears. Turn, then, most gracious advocate, thy eyes of mercy towards us, and after this our exile is ended, show unto us the blessed fruit of thy womb, Jesus, O clement, O pious, O sweet Virgin Mary." Now, is it not a farce to call this Christianity? It is a great deal more like *atheism*. Here is an authorized Catholic prayer, in which there is no recognition of God whatever!

Then follows a call to devout contemplation, and one would suppose that the object of it would be God, or the Savior. But no, it is the Virgin. "Let us, with exultation, contemplate the blessed Virgin Mary sitting in glory at the right hand of her beloved Son. She is crowned by the heavenly Father queen of heaven and earth, and appointed by Jesus Christ the dispenser of his graces." It is singular that the Catholics, when they look up to heaven, see no object so conspicuous as the blessed Virgin. Now, she was not the most prominent figure in those visions of heaven of which we have account in the Bible. *Stephen* saw "the heavens opened, and the Son of man standing on the right hand of God," but he saw nothing of the Virgin Mary sitting at her Son's right hand. Nor does *John*, in the history he gives in the book of Revelation of his visions of heaven, make any mention of seeing her. But it seems she is not only visible to the contemplative Catholic, but almost alone conspicuous.

They speak of her moreover as crowned universal queen, and appointed dispenser of the graces of Christ. But where did they get that information? It is too much to expect us to take their word for it, since it is acknowledged that we have not the word of God for it. I always supposed Christ to be, through his Spirit, the dispenser of his own graces. I always understood it to be him who "received gifts for men." But it seems, according to the Catholics, that quite a different person received and dispenses them. How much *novelty* there is in the Catholic religion! It is almost all of it comparatively new doctrine. Ours, the Protestant, is the *old* religion, after all that is said to the contrary.

But the Catholic is so positive in regard to the coronation of the blessed Virgin, that we find him using the following thanksgiving, "O Jesus, in union with angels and saints, I bless thee for the glory with which thou hast environed thy holy mother, and I give thee thanks from the bottom of my heart, for having given her to me, for my queen, my protectress and my mother." Here ends the thanksgiving to Jesus. They soon become weary of addressing him, and fondly return to the mother. "O queen of angels and men, grant thy powerful intercession to those who are united to honor thee in the confraternity of the holy rosary," (I don't know what that means; it is a mystery that I must leave unexplained), "and to all thy other servants." Then follows something to which I solicit particular attention. I suspect the author and approvers of the book would be glad to obliterate the sentence I am going to quote, if they could. But it is too late. The words are these: "I consecrate myself entirely to thy service." Here the person wishing to be guided to heaven is directed, under the authority of the archbishop, to consecrate himself entirely to the service of the Virgin Mary, who is acknowledged on all hands to be a creature. Mark, it is *entirely*. This excludes God altogether from any share in the person's services. He is to be *entirely* consecrated to the service of the Virgin. Will anyone, who has any regard for his character as an intelligent being, say that this is not idolatry? There cannot be a plainer case of idolatry made out in any part of the world, or from any portion of history. St. Paul beseeches us to present our bodies a living sacrifice to God, which, he says, is our reasonable service; but this Catholic guide to heaven directs us to consecrate ourselves entirely to the service of the Virgin Mary.

Accordingly, the docile Catholic does consecrate himself to Mary, as in the following act of devotion to her, which you may read in the same little book: "O blessed Virgin, I come to offer thee my most humble homage, and to implore the aid of thy prayers and protection. Thou art all-powerful with the Almighty. Thou knowest that from my tender years I looked up to thee as my mother, my advocate, and patroness. Thou wert pleased to consider me from that time as one of thy children. I will henceforth serve, honor and love thee. Accept my protestation of fidelity; look favorably on the confidence I have in thee; obtain for me, of thy dear Son, a lively faith; a firm hope; a tender, generous, and constant love, that I may experience the power of thy protection at my death." Here you perceive the Catholic says he will do what "the guide" directs him to do. He will serve her, and so doing, he hopes to experience the power of her protection at his death. Poor soul! I pity him, if he has no better company in death than that. That was not the reason David said, "Though I walk through the valley of the shadow of death, I will fear no evil." His reason was, "for Thou [the Lord, his shepherd] art with me; thy rod and thy staff, they comfort me." How can Mary be with every dying Catholic who trusts in her? I should like to know. Do they go so far as to say she is omnipresent? Have they *formally* deified her, as *in fact* they have?

The devotee in this prayer uses the following language to the Virgin: "Thou art all-powerful with the Almighty." Shall I call this an *error* or a *falsehood?* It is certain that there is no truth in it. She, a poor sinful creature, like the rest of us, saved by grace, all-powerful with the Almighty in intercession! Christ is that; but no other being is; and to say that any other is, is not only falsehood, but *blasphemy.*

I have other specimens of Catholic idolatry, which I mean to give; but those I have exhibited are sufficient to convict that church of idolatry before any court that ever sat, or any jury that was ever impanneled. *I have proved the Catholic church and religion to be idolatrous.* I have not merely asserted it, it has been *demonstrated*, and the proof has been taken from her own authorized publication. To have *said* she was idolatrous, would have been uncharitable. To have *proved* it, is not. A man is responsible for the drift of his assertions, but not for the scope of his arguments.

Idolatrous! Yes, she who pretends to be the only church,

is convicted, out of her own mouth, of idolatry. She has this millstone about her neck. I wonder she has *swum* with it so long. It must *sink* her presently. I think I see her *going down* already, although I know many suppose she is rising in the world.

CHAPTER TWENTY-THREE
More Specimens of Catholic Idolatry

———————◆◇◆———————

Why, reader, did you know that the Catholics not only *pray* to the Virgin Mary, but *sing* to her? I was not aware of it until I got hold of the book I have been reviewing. But it is a fact that they do. At the end of the book I find the two following *hymns* addressed to her. They are both in common metre. Here is the *first*. You will see that, in point of idolatry, they are fully up to the prayers to her.

> O holy mother of our God,
> To thee for help we fly;
> Despise not this our humble prayer,
> But all our wants supply.
>
> O glorious virgin, ever blest,
> Defend us from our foes;
> From threatening dangers set us free,
> And terminate our woes.

Here is the idolatry of looking to a creature for *the supply of all wants,* and of flying to a creature for help and for defence. There is a curse pronounced in Jeremiah 17:5, on the man "that trusteth in man, and maketh flesh his arm." If the person who devoutly uses this hymn does not make "flesh his arm," I should like to know who does.

The other hymn runs thus:

> Hail, Mary, queen and virgin pure,
> With every grace replete;
> Hail, kind protectress of the poor,
> Pity our needy state.
>
> O thou who fill'st the highest place,
> Next heaven's imperial throne;
> Obtain for us each saving grace,
> And make our wants thy own.
>
> How oft, when trouble filled my breast,
> Or sin my conscience pained,
> Through thee I sought for peace and rest,
> Through thee I peace obtained.
>
> Then hence, in all my pains and cares,
> I'll seek for help in thee;
> E'er trusting, through thy powerful prayers,
> To gain eternity.

But it seems the blessed Virgin is not the only creature they *sing* to. I find in the same book a hymn to *St. Joseph,* of which the first verse is,

> Holy Patron, thee saluting,
> Here we meet with hearts sincere;
> Blest St. Joseph, all uniting,
> Call on thee to hear our prayer.

Perhaps the reader is aware that the Catholics are not satisfied with praying merely to *animated* beings, they sometimes supplicate things which have no life. Indeed they seem disposed to worship almost everything, except it be him whom alone they should worship. To give but one example, I find in "the Litany of the blessed Sacrament," as they call it, among many other similar supplications, this one, "O wheat of the elect, have mercy on us." What a prayer this, to be sanctioned by an archbishop, and sent forth from one of the most enlightened cities of America, and that in the nineteenth century too! It is really too bad. We talk of the *progress* of things. But here is *retrocession* with a witness. In the *first* century the rule was, according to the practice of the publican, to pray "God be merciful to me a sinner;" but now in the *nineteenth,* the sinner is directed to say, "wheat of the elect, have mercy on us!"

I think we have found, with reference to the Catholic religion, what *Archimedes* could not find when he wanted to move the world. He said he could move it, provided he could have a place to stand on, from which he could with his lever act upon the world. But as no such place could be found for him, the world was not moved. I think, however, that I have discovered a spot from which we can not only move, but utterly subvert the Roman Catholic religion. We pass over her absurdity and her intolerance, and plant ourselves on her *idolatry.* Here we will stand, and from this place we will carry on our operations against her. If the Roman Catholic church is idolatrous, can she stand? Must she not fall? What! a church that is plainly idolatrous maintain its ground as the church of Christ! It is impossible. It is but for the eyes of mankind to be opened to see her idolatry, and her reign is over. The common sense of the world cannot long brook prayers and hymns to creatures, and supplications for mercy to that of which bread is made. I would not have it persecuted; I would not have one of its adherents harmed in the slightest degree; but there are some things which the enlightened intellect of man cannot tolerate; and this is the chief of those things which are intolerable to reason. It must go off the stage, even though infidelity should come on and occupy it. The religion that is not of the Bible, and that scoffs at reason, must come to an end. I have no fears of its rising to any higher ascendancy than that it now occupies. My hope is in God; but if it were not, it would be in *man*.

CHAPTER TWENTY-FOUR
Image Worship

If there be any truth in phrenology, I judge that Catholics must have the organ of veneration very largely developed. There are no people, unless it be some Pagans, who are so inclined to worship. They worship almost everything that comes in their way; with scarcely any discrimination. The value of worship with them seems to depend on the variety of objects worshiped. What a pity it is they cannot confine their worship within narrower bounds! What a pity they are not satisfied with one object of religious veneration – the great and glorious God! But no. Besides him, they must have a host of creatures, angels, saints, and what not, as objects of adoration. Nor are they satisfied with these beings themselves. They must have visible representations of them to bow down unto, and worship. They want something to worship which they can *see*. In the profession of faith which I find in the little book published in Baltimore under the sanction of the archbishop, from which I have quoted so freely already, and to which I love to appeal, seeing it is published so near home, and there can be no dispute about its authority, I find this paragraph among others: "I most firmly assert, that the *images* of Christ, of the mother of God, ever Virgin, and also of the saints, ought to be had and retained, and that due honor and veneration is to be given them." This doctrine sounds a little different from that promulgated from Sinai, and written with the finger of God on the tables of stone. They *look* to be at variance, to say the least; and I think I shall be able to show presently that they have that *aspect* to Catholics as well as Protestants. The voice that shook the earth, after saying, "Thou shalt have no other gods before me," said, "Thou shalt not *make* unto thee any graven image, or any likeness of any thing that is in heaven above," &c.

Now Christ, the Virgin, and the saints are in heaven above, unless any choose to surmise that some of those reckoned saints are elsewhere. Consequently no likeness of them may be made. The law proceeds: "Thou shalt not bow down thyself to them, nor serve them." But do not Catholics bow down or *kneel* before likenesses of the saints and others? I ask the question. I know they used to do so, and I suppose I may infer that they do so now, since it is their grand boast that their religion is *everywhere and always the same*. The doctrine delivered from Sinai is the old notion on the subject, and it would seem to be against every kind and degree of image worship. But, says the modern "guide to heaven," what the authoritative Council of Trent had said many years before, "the images of Christ, of the mother of God, and also of the saints, ought to be had and retained, and due honor and venera-tion given them." Here are *Baltimore* and *Trent* against *Sinai;* or, in other words, the archbishop and council on one side, and he who came down on the mountain which burned with fire on the other. My hearers must range themselves on either side, as they see fit.

But cannot the two things be reconciled somehow? Can they not be so *explained* as to remove all appearance of incon-sistency? Perhaps they can, if one of them be explained *away,* that is, be made so clear that you can't see it any longer. This is a new way some have of reconciling things; but I, as an individual, do not think much of it. I like the old way of laying things alongside of each other, and then shedding as much light as possible on both. If this is done with the two things in question, I fear there is no hope of reconciling them. To this conclusion our Catholic brethren themselves seem to have come; and seeing that the two things could not be so explained as to appear in harmony, they have most effectually explained one of them *away*. They have *suppressed* it. The second commandment has been thrown out of the Decalogue, as I have shown on a former occasion. This is a part of the Catholics' "short and easy method with Protestants." It beats Leslie's with the Deists all to nothing. Whether it be as *honest* and *correct* a method, as it is short and easy, I refer to the judgment of my readers. One thing is very certain; the Catholics must think that the old second commandment *is,* or at least *looks* very much against them, otherwise they would not have meddled with it. Can any other reason be given for the suppression of the second commandment, but that it seems to forbid that use which Catholics make of images in their churches? If anybody can imagine another reason, I will thank him to state it. Now, where there can be but one motive impelling to an act, I suppose it is not uncharitable to refer the act to that motive.

I believe the reader is aware that, even in the little modern Baltimore book, "the guide to heaven," the second commandment is suppressed. I think I have stated that fact in a former article. It is so. And why should it not be? Why should not the *invariable* religion be the same here that it is in Ireland or Italy? Why should American Catholics be bound to keep one more commandment than European Catholics? Why should they of the old countries have greater liberty of action than we of the new world? The circumstances under which the second commandment is omitted in "the guide to," &c., are these. An examination, preparatory to confession, is recommended to the devout Catholic, on the ten commandments, that he may see, before he goes to the priest to get forgiveness, wherein he has transgressed any of them. Now, he is not directed to examine himself on the second, but *twice over* on the tenth, so as to make out the full number. Now I acknowledge it would have been awkward to have set the person to examining himself in reference to the second commandment. It might have led to a conviction of sins not recognized by his confessor. If he had asked himself, "is there any graven image, or likeness of any thing in heaven above, or in the earth beneath, to which I bow down?" himself would have been apt to answer, "Why yes, there is that image of Christ I kneel before – and there is that likeness of the blessed Virgin I bow down to and adore – I am afraid I have broken the second commandment." If then he had gone to the priest with his scruples, you see it would have made work and trouble. It is true, the priest could have said to him, "O, my child, you don't mean anything by it. You only use the image as a help to devotion. Your worship does not terminate on it. Your worship of it is only *relative*. Besides, you don't *adore* the image – you only *venerate* it – and you only give *'due* honor and veneration' to images – nothing more than that. You should consider, my child, the distinction be-tween adoration and veneration – and also between *latria* and *dulia."* But this might not have satisfied the person's con-science. It might have been all *Greek* to him. Wherefore it was judged most prudent not to recommend any examination on the commandment about images. Perhaps it was the more prudent course. The *policy* of the measure I do not dispute.

But, say the Catholics, have not Protestants their pictures and statues? Certainly we have. We do not make war against the fine arts. We can approve of *painting* and *statuary* without practicing *idolatry*. Yes, we have representations of deceased Christians, but we do not kneel before them, nor do we on that account drop the second commandment, as some do. The Catholics make a great many explanations and distinctions on this subject of image worship, some of which I have adverted to above, in what I have supposed the priest to say. But they are substantially the same that the ancient Israelite might have made, and the modern Pagan makes in justification of himself. Idolaters, when called upon to explain themselves, have al-ways been in the habit of saying that it was only a *relative* worship they paid to the visible object, and that the adoration was meant to pass through and terminate on an invisible object beyond. This explanation is not original with the modern Christian idolater. It is as old as Jewish and Pagan idolatry. The worshipers of the golden calf worshiped something *beyond* the calf. The calf was only a help to devotion, and they only paid "due honor and veneration" to it. Nevertheless they "sinned a great sin," and "the Lord plagued the people" on account of it. "There fell of the people that day about 3,000." I suppose it would have been just the same had they made ever so many explanations. But their explanations were not waited for. What signifies all these explanations and distinctions to the great mass of the Catholic laity? They do not even understand them; and it seems that if they both understood and regarded them, it would not help the matter. It is this very explained and qualified worship which the commandment forbids.

I have nothing more to say about images, but I wish the Archbishop of Baltimore would allow the second commandment to appear in the next edition of the *Guide to Heaven*. I wish he would let the publisher's stereotype plates be altered so as to conform to the tables of stone. I am afraid the people will not get to heaven if they have not respect to *all* God's commandments. The Psalmist seems to have thought that necessary. Ps. 119:6. It would gratify me much, if the archbishop would permit the Lord to say to his people all he has to say.

CHAPTER TWENTY-FIVE
Relics

My last was on the subject of images. Here are some more things to which the Catholics, if they do not exactly worship them, pay a respect and veneration which is very apt to run into worship. They are *relics,* so called. I have just come from the dictionary where I went to find the word. I consulted *Cruden's Concordance* first, but I found no such word there. That contains only the words which are used in the Bible. Relics came in fashion after the Bible was written. In those old times they were not in the habit of mutilating the bodies and disturbing the bones of the pious dead. They respected the remains of the departed by letting them alone, as king Josiah ordered the people to do in the case of the bones of the two prophets. They were going to disturb them, but he told them to let them alone, 2 Kings 23:18. This is the way in which Protestants respect the remains of the dead. It is rather queer that Catholics, in the lack of other Scripture to support their doctrine of relics, appeal to this, and they will have it that Josiah, like themselves, entertained a great respect for relics. The reference to that passage must be on the principle of *lucus, a non lucendo* (light from no light). I cannot account for it in any other way.

By the way, I did not even find relics in the concordance

to the Apocrypha. But Johnson has it. A dictionary, you know, takes in all words. I find the general signification of the word to be *remains*. In the Catholic church it is used to designate "the remains of the bodies, or clothes, of saints or martyrs, and the instruments by which they were put to death, devoutly preserved, in honor to their memory; kissed, revered, and carried in procession." This is the best definition of relics I can any where find. I am indebted for it to the Encyclopedia. But it is not a perfect definition. There are some things presented and revered as relics which don't exactly fall under it; as, for example, the rope with which Judas hanged himself, and the tail of Balaam's ass, both of which are kept and shown as relics.

But it may be asked if relics are not out of date. The inquirer should know that nothing ever gets out of date with the Catholics. *Always and everywhere the same* is their boast respecting their religion. Besides, in the Baltimore publication, the *Guide to Heaven*, notice is taken of relics. It says that the saints are to be honored and invocated, and that their relics are to be respected. Well, and where is the harm of respecting relics? I might retaliate and ask where is the *use* – what is the good of it? They must think that devotion is promoted by these relics. But I cannot see how the spirit of devotion is to be promoted by contemplating St. Joseph's axe and saw, or the comb of the Virgin Mary, or even the finger of St. Ann. If a person even knows that he is handling a piece of the identical wood of the cross, it does not occur to me how that is to enkindle the flame of piety in his heart. The ancient method of exciting the glow of devotion was quite different. It was by meditation on spiritual subjects. It was while the Psalmist was *musing,* that "the fire burned" within him. But it seems the Catholics come to the same thing by the aid of their relics. Well, if devotion is kindled by relics, towards whom does it flame? Towards the saints, to be sure, whose relics they are. These remains can only remind them of those to whom they once belonged. So that it is the religious veneration of saints, not the worship of Jehovah, that is promoted by relics. All that

that they serve the cause of idolatry. can be said for them is,
    But I have been writing as if these relics were genuine
remains of the saints – the saw they show really St. Joseph's,
and the finger St. Ann's. The reader must excuse me for in-
dulging such a supposition. The very idea of such things being
preserved, and transmitted through eighteen centuries, is
preposterous. Their own writers acknowledge that many of
them are spurious – that bones are often consecrated, which,
so far from belonging to saints, probably did not belong to
Christians, if indeed to human beings. If this be so, how are we
to know which are genuine? There can be no internal evidence
to distinguish them. The bones of saints must look just like
other bones. I know it is said there is an odor about the genuine relics which does not belong to the remains of the vulgar
dead. How that is I cannot say. I understand that, in the failure
of the ordinary, external evidence, the Pope takes it on him to
pronounce them genuine. This is making short work of it. But
some of the authorities of the church of Rome go so far as to
say that it is not necessary the relics should be genuine. It is
enough that the worshiper has an intention of honoring the
saints whose bones he supposes them to be. If this is correct
doctrine, churches and chapels may be readily furnished with
relics, and the defect in this particular, which Catholics de-
plore in regard to many of their establishments, be supplied
without going farther than the nearest graveyard.
    If anyone should still think that the relics may be genuine,
there is a consideration which, if I mistake not, will carry
complete conviction to his mind. It is, that there are altogether
too many of these relics, so that some of them must be spurious. Five devout pilgrims happening to meet on their return
from Rome, found, on comparing their notes, that each had
been honored with a foot of the very ass upon which Christ
rode to Jerusalem. Here were five feet for one animal. Moreover, it is said that there are as many pieces of the timber of
the true cross in different parts of Europe, as would supply a
town with fuel for a winter!

But, say they, were not the bones of Joseph preserved, and afterwards removed to Canaan? Undoubtedly they were. But they were all kept together in a coffin, and they were removed, not to be worshiped, but to be buried. Joseph, being persuaded that God would visit his people, and bring them out of Egypt into Canaan, enjoined it on them to take his remains along with them, for he wished them to repose in the land of promise. What this has to do with relics I have not the discernment to perceive. How it bears any resemblance to the Catholic practice of disturbing coffins and separating bone from bone, and cherishing them as things to be revered, I cannot see. Yet no less a character than Cardinal Bellarmine appeals to this fact in support of their doctrine of relics. So also they cite the case recorded in 2 Kings 13:21, of the dead man that was revived by coming in contact with the bones of Elisha. But how does this favor relics? The bones of Elisha were quietly reposing in the place where they were laid at his death. Not one of them had been touched. But if relics had been in vogue then, do you suppose the remains of such an eminent saint as Elisha would have been left undisturbed?

I was surprised to find that Bellarmine refers to Deut. 31:6 in support of relics. It is that remarkable passage in which the Lord is said to have buried Moses in a valley in the land of Moab, and that no man knoweth of his sepulchre unto this day. I suppose the cardinal would have us infer from this, that if the place of Moses' body had been known, it would have been dug up and converted into relics. And therefore the Lord took care it should not be known. The devil, it seems, from Jude 5:9, contended for it for some such purpose as this, but he was foiled. The reference to this passage strikes me as rather an unhappy one.

But were not handkerchiefs and aprons brought from the body of Paul, and miracles thereby wrought? Yes, but they were not relics. Paul was living. Besides, who does not see that those articles of dress were but *signs* to connect the miracles, in the minds of the people, with the person of God's inspired ambassador? Was any honor due to them? Do we hear of their being preserved and revered? No. I do not find them in any list of relics. They passed again immediately into their former appropriate use as handkerchiefs and aprons. Finally, they appeal to the efficacy of the shadow of Peter, as related in Acts 5:15, in proof of the virtue of relics. But as there appears to be no *substance* in this argument, I leave it unanswered; and have only to add, that I wonder not that infidels abound so in Catholic countries, when Christianity is held up before them as embracing and even giving prominence to such doctrines as the veneration of relics, the invocation of saints, and many more like them.

CHAPTER TWENTY-SIX
Seven Sacraments

What! Seven! How is this? I read in the Bible of only *two*. Whence have they the other *five?* O, they come from the other source of Christian doctrine, *tradition*. They were *handed* down. It is true, the apostles wrote of only two sacraments; but Catholics would have us believe that they *preached* and *conversed* about five others: and those that heard them spoke of these sacraments to others; and they to others still; and so the story passed from lip to lip, until the Council of Trent, I believe it was, concluded that something had better be written about these five *extra* sacraments. I wonder that was never thought of before. It is surprising that it never occurred to the apostles, when they were writing their Epistles, to say a syllable about these seven sacraments. It would seem to have been very thoughtless in them. I may be very hard to please, but I cannot help feeling a desire to have *Scripture,* as well as *unwritten tradition,* in support of a doctrine or practice called Christian. I like to be able to trace a doctrine all the way back to the Bible, and to find it originating in the very oracles of God themselves. Some think it sufficient, if they can follow a doctrine back as far as the earlier fathers; and especially if they can trace it to the Epistles of Ignatius. But this does not satisfy me. There are certain other Epistles, rather more an-

cient, in which I would like to find the doctrine. Ignatius was
a very good man, but he did not belong to the days of Paul by
any means. Ignatius, Clemens, and all those good fathers,
stood on the bank of the stream, but Paul and his associates sat
around the fountain. These last saw truth in its rise; the others
only saw it in its flow. True, they were near the source, but
they were not *at* it; and who knows not that a stream may be
corrupted very near its source? If I live eighteen or nineteen
miles distant from a certain fountain, whose stream passes by
my residence, and I want to know whether its waters have been
corrupted, do I trace back the stream until I come within a mile
or two of the fountain, and there stop, concluding that such as
the water is there, such it must be at the spring? Do I not rather
go all the way up to the fountain? Which ought I to do? It
strikes me as very strange, that any should suspend their search
after truth a century or two this side of the Bible era. I think
they should go all the way back to the Bible.

But I am wandering from my subject, which is the sacraments. What are those other *five?* One is *marriage.* What!
marriage a sacrament! How does it answer to the definition of
sacrament? What spiritual thing is signified by it? Marriage
is said to be "honorable in all," but nothing is said of its being
a sacrament. If it be a sacrament, why are not priests, as well
as others, permitted to *take* this sacrament? Why should the
universal clergy be debarred the privilege of this holy thing?
Does its *sacred* character render it unsuitable to those who fill
the sacred office?

The other day I was thinking – for, being a Protestant, I
dare think even on religion – and this thought occurred to me:
"Is it possible that God has denied the whole body of the
clergy, of all nations and ages, the privilege of knowing how
he pitieth them that fear him; and of approaching to the experi-
mental knowledge of his exceeding readiness to give the Holy
Spirit to them that ask him – the privilege, in other words, of
being able to feel the force of some of the most touching
representations which he has made of his dispositions towards

his creatures, founded on the parental relation?" I read in the Bible that "like as a *father* pitieth his children, *so* the Lord pitieth them that fear him." Now, can it be sinful for a minister of Jesus Christ to know by experience (the only way in which it can be fully known) how a father pitieth, and how, consequently, the Lord pitieth his people? I think it is man, and not God, that constitutes this a sin. Again, does God make this general appeal to his creatures, "If ye then, being evil, know how to give good gifts unto your children, how much more shall your heavenly Father give the Holy Spirit to them that ask him!" – and has he at the same time excluded a large class of his creatures from the privilege of ever knowing how well disposed parents are to bestow good things on their children? And has he laid under this ban the very persons whom he has appointed to represent and testify of him to men? Has he appealed to the parental feelings of his creatures, and then forbidden a large and important class of them to know what those feelings are? This is rather more than I can believe.

A minister of Jesus Christ may decline the privilege of marriage in his own case – he may not use that *power,* as Paul, in his peculiar circumstances, did not, and as many a *Protestant* minister does not. This is one thing; but has God cut off the whole order of the clergy from even the *right* to marry? That is the question. And that is a very different thing.

CHAPTER TWENTY-SEVEN
Transubstantiation

———◆———

Because Christ says, in reference to the bread, "This is my body," the Catholics contend that the bread is changed into the body of Christ; and this they call Transubstantiation. And when we say that the passage is not to be interpreted *literally,* but that the bread is merely indicated as the representative of Christ's body, they reply with wonderful confidence, "Ah, but does he not say it is his body – does he say it *represents* his body merely – what authority have Protestants to bring in a figure here?" Now let me be heard. I have no disposition to ridicule the doctrine of Transubstantiation, especially as it professes to be founded on Scripture. I would give always a candid hearing to the claims of a doctrine which even seems to be held out of respect to the authority of the Bible. But I must say that the Catholic does not carry his veneration for the Scriptures far enough; or he is not consistent in his interpretation of them. I think I can show that, to be consistent with himself, he should believe in many more than one Transubstantiation. Let him turn to Luke 22:19-20. He reads in verse 19, "This is my body." Therefore, he reasons, the bread becomes the body of Christ. Very well. But read verse 20: "This cup is the new testament." Here is another Transubstantiation. The cup or chalice becomes the new testament. It is no longer *gold* or *silver,* but a testament or *will!* Does not Christ say it *is* the new testament? What right have *Catholics* to bring in *figure* here? *The cup is a will* – Christ says so. To be sure, if it were carried to a probate office, it would be thought out of place, and an article for a silversmith to prove, rather than a judge of probate. But no matter for that. What if the senses do tell you that it is still a cup, and the body still bread, will you believe those liars, the senses? But if they are such liars as this would make them out to be, why should I ever believe them – why should I believe them, when they tell me that I see in the Bible those words: "This is my body?" That testimony of the senses the Catholic believes; but if they lie about the body, still declaring it is bread, after it has ceased to be any such thing, why may they not lie in regard to the letters which spell "this is my body." Under the appearance of these letters there may be something quite different, even as, under the appearance of bread in the Eucharist, is the body of Christ, as the Catholics affirm!

But these are not the only instances of Transubstantiation. The Bible is full of them. I find two cases of this *change* recorded in Revelation 1:20; *one* in which certain stars become angels, and another in which certain candlesticks become churches. Do you doubt it? Read for yourself: "The seven stars *are* the angels of the seven churches, and the seven candlesticks which thou sawest, *are* the seven churches." The construction here is precisely similar to "this is my body." Christ *is* the speaker in each case, and he says the stars *are* angels, and the candlesticks *are* churches. Who has any right to imagine a *figure* here?

Perhaps everybody does not know that Transubstantiation is an Old Testament doctrine. But, according to this mode of interpretation, it is St. Paul, in 1 Cor. 10:4, alluding to the rock which Moses smote in the wilderness, says, "That rock was Christ" – not it *represented,* but it *was* Christ! Away with your figures.

Many other examples of Transubstantiation might be given

given from the Old Testament. Let two remarkable cases suffice, of which we have an account in Genesis 41:26-27: "The seven good kine are seven years, and the seven good ears are seven years," &c. Here seven cows and seven ears of corn are changed into seven years of three hundred and sixty-five days each!

I suppose I might find many hundred examples of these Transubstantiations. Now, does the Catholic believe in all of them? He ought, most undoubtedly he ought, on the same reason that he believes in one. Let him then either believe in them all, or else never adduce, "this *is* my body," in proof of the Transubstantiation held in his church. I wish Mr. H. or somebody else would set me right, if I err in this argument.

CHAPTER TWENTY-EIGHT
Half a Sacrament

Half a sacrament! Who ever heard of such a thing? A sacrament divided! Yes, even so. The authorities of the Roman Catholic church, Pope, Council, &c., have divided the sacrament of the Lord's Supper, which our Savior instituted the same night in which he was betrayed; and, ever since the Council of Constance, they have allowed the people only half of it.

They have told them that they must put up with the bread, for that they want the cup for themselves. But did not Christ give the cup, in the original institution of the sacrament, to as many as he gave the bread? Yes, *Christ* did. So say Matthew, Mark, Luke, and Paul. He took the cup, they tell us, and gave it to them; and Matthew adds that he said in giving it, "Drink ye *all* of it." Let not this be omitted by any disciple. It would seem as if Christ foresaw what the Constance Council was going to do, and therefore said, "Drink ye all of it." Rome might with more plausibility have denied her laity the other half of the sacrament – the bread. After the command to take the cup, there follows the reason; observe it: "For this is my blood of the new testament, which is shed for *many,* for the remission of sins." Now the Catholics say that only priests were present on that occasion, and that the giving of the cup to them can be no precedent for giving it to the laity. But, though we should admit that they were at that time priests, I want to know if the reason for partaking of the cup does not apply to others besides the clergy. Was not the blood shed for the laity as well as for the clergy? And if this is the reason why any should partake, it is equally a reason why all should for whom the blood was shed. The precept and privilege to drink is co-extensive with the reason annexed to it. Now I have not been in the habit of regarding the propitiatory death of Christ as a part of the *benefit of clergy* – as one of the peculiar privileges of the priesthood. I object therefore to the restriction of the cup of blessing to the clergy. The symbol of the blood shed for many, for the remission of sins, I claim to be my privilege as truly as that of any priest. Christ did not shed his blood for the sons of Levi alone.

Yes, Christ, gave it in both kinds – and what is more, the Catholics themselves acknowledge that he did, and that the primitive church administered it in both kinds, yet *(hoc tamen non obstante* are their very words) they appoint that the people shall receive it but in one kind, that is, notwithstanding Christ and the primitive church. And they declare them accursed who teach or practice otherwise. What is this but *anathematizing* Christ? But surely they must have something to say in justification of their conduct in this respect. To be sure they have. Do you not know that the Pope is the head of the church, and that he is infallible; or if he is not, yet the *firm* Pope & Co. are? Yes, but there was Pope *Gelasius,* who lived a good while be-fore. He having heard of some Manicheans who received the bread without the wine, decided that such a dividing of one and the same sacrament might not be done without a heinous sacrilege. Was not he head of the church too, and was not he infallible? If he was not, I wonder how he could transmit infallibility.

This withholding of the cup is one of the *boldest strokes* of that church. I cannot help admiring the *courage* it manifests. Who would have thought it could have succeeded so well? I wonder they even undertook to carry this point. However, they have done it. There was some murmuring against it, to be sure. *Huss* and *Jerome* made a noise about it, but they just burnt them, and they made no more noise about it.

But are not Christians *followers,* that is, *imitators* of Christ? O yes. But this withholding of the cup is not doing like Christ. The Catholics say that Christ is with their church to the *end* of time. It strikes me, however, that he could not have been with them at that point in the progress of time when the Council of Constance sat.

I do not know what others think, but for my own part I don't believe that any power on earth has a right to limit a grant of Jesus Christ, or, in other words, to take away what he has given. He said of the cup, "drink ye *all* of it" – and I, for one, will do it, and I think all ought – and if the Catholics will come over to us, they too shall have the cup of salvation. O, if I had the ear of the Catholics now, I would not ask them to confess their sins to me, but there is a thing I would tell them: I would say, My dear Catholic brethren, you never remember Christ in his sacrament. You only *half* remember him. He said, eat and drink in remembrance of me. You only do one. You do not *show* the Lord's death; for Paul says, "as often as ye eat this bread *and* drink this cup, ye do show the Lord's death." It is only they who do *both* that make this exhibition. Christ's death is not shown by the bread merely, but by both the elements. I know your church says that the blood is in the body, and that, in taking one, both are taken, for that "Christ was entire and truly under each kind," as the council decrees. But how came Christ himself to know nothing of this? Did he do a superfluous thing in giving the cup? What if the blood is in the body, and the bread being changed into the body we take the one in taking the other, we want the blood *separated* from the body, the blood *shed.* The blood of Christ is not an atonement for sin, except as it is shed. Catholics, you never celebrate the Lord's Supper. In the Lord's Supper there was a *cup.* In yours there is none. You hold that the discourse in John 6, relates to an atonement, and there it is written, "except ye eat the flesh of the Son of man, and drink his blood, ye have no life in you." Now, according to his own principles, you have no life in you, for you do not *drink* his blood. The most you can be said to do is, that you eat it in connection with his body! One thing more, Catholic brethren. There can be no such thing in reality as half a sacrament. To divide a sacrament is to destroy it. What follows then but that the whole sacrament is taken from you! Look at this – just fix your mind five minutes on this subject, and you are, I do not say what, but you are no longer a Catholic. *Five minutes.* That is all. But you say, I must not *doubt;* yet you may *think,* and God the judge will never condemn you for exercising your mind.

CHAPTER TWENTY-NINE
Extreme Unction

———————◆◇◆———————

When it looks as if one was going to die, then by all means let the priest be sent for: and when he has come, let him receive the dying man's confession (but if the priest should be long in coming, I would advise him to confess to God. I think it would answer as well. Indeed I prefer that near way to pardon, to the other circuitous route) – and let him then in that extremity anoint him with oil! This is *extreme unction* – a sacrament – one of the *seven!* I think they must have been at a loss to make up the seven, when they pressed this into the service.

There does not seem to be a great deal of religion in it; nor indeed any excess of common sense. But to speak of it as constituting a preparation for death is really shocking. What! a preparation for dying, and for meeting and answering to God, procured by the intervention and unction of a human priest done by oil! Truly this is an easy way of getting to heaven, particularly where priests are plenty. I do not wonder that the Catholic religion is *popular*. This is indeed prophesying *smooth* things. We Protestants have no such doctrine to preach. When we are called to see a sick person, we candidly acknowledge that there is nothing *we* can do for him which shall infallibly secure his salvation. We tell him what he must

do: that he must repent and believe in Christ: and then we ask
God to undertake and do for him. It is only on certain conditions that we can assure him of his salvation. The priests say
that they can *insure* the person's salvation; but to any such
power as that we do not pretend.

But have not the Catholics plain Scripture for their doctrine of extreme unction? If they have; if it is *written,* and not
merely *handed down,* then I am at once a believer in it. Let us
see: they adduce two passages in support of their dogma, Mark
6:13, and James 5:14. The first is *historical.* It affirms that the
apostles "anointed with oil many that were sick and healed
them." The other is *hortatory.* "Is any sick among you? let him
call for the elders of the church; and let them pray over him,
anointing him with oil in the name of the Lord," that is, doing
what the apostles are represented by Mark as having done; and
doing it, as appears from the next verse, with the same end in
view, viz. *healing.* Now, what authority for the sacrament of
extreme unction is there here? Here is indeed an anointing
with oil by an ecclesiastic. But who does not see in how many
particulars, and how widely this anointing differs from the
extreme unction of the Catholics? Their anointing proceeds on
the supposition that the person is going to die; and could his
recovery be foreseen, it would be omitted. But the anointing
practiced by the apostles and elders of the church was in order
to the recovery of the person, and was in every case connected
with his recovery. Their anointing was the *attendant* and *token*
of a miraculous cure. It held precisely the same place with
Christ's making clay of spittle, and anointing therewith the
eyes of the blind man; or with Naaman's being directed to go
and wash seven times in Jordan. It was, like each of these, an
external, and in itself inefficacious sign of a miraculous recovery; and even now there is no objection to the use of the sign,
if the thing signified is to be expected. Let the priests anoint
with abundance of oil all their sick, if they can accompany that
unction with such a prayer of faith as shall save the sick. But
if the miraculous recoveries have ceased, let there be a doing
away of the sign. As soon as any sign becomes *insignificant,*

let it cease to be used. Extreme unction is now a sign of *nothing*. There was no use in going down into the pool of Bethesda after the angel had ceased to pay his periodical visit to it. So in this case, there being now no healing, there need be, and there should be, no anointing.

How the priests now differ in their use of the oil from those whose successors they pretend to be! The apostles and elders anointed persons with a view to their living; but the priests with a view to their *dying*. The former would not anoint, if they foresaw the person was to die; the latter will not, if they foresee that he is to live. How at odds they are! How Scripture and tradition do quarrel! And the worst of it is, there is no such thing as bringing about a reconciliation between them.

Among the doctrines of the Catholic church, I am at a loss whether to give the palm to this or to purgatory. Purgatory teaches the doctrine of salvation by *fire*. Extreme unction, the doctrine of salvation by *oil*. There does not seem to be much Christianity in either. Extreme unction is, however, the *smoothest* doctrine. Decidedly so. Jesus Christ came by *water* and *blood*. The salvation he proclaims is by *these;* and the sacraments he instituted, are Baptism and the Lord's Supper. These signify something: the first, *regeneration;* the second, the *propitiation* made for our sins.

CHAPTER THIRTY
Doing Penance

Insufferable! What? Why, that the Catholic translators of the Bible should render the Greek word, which signifies *repentance (metanoia)*, by the phrase *doing penance!* I would not willingly be uncharitable, imputing a bad motive where a good one might have been present. But I must say that I know not how to reconcile this rendering of *metanoia* with their integrity as translators. I cannot help believing that they knew better. Could they have supposed that they were selecting the most judicious method of conveying the mind of the Spirit as expressed in that word, when they concluded on rendering it *doing penance?* Why, in the name of common sense, did they use *two* English words (coining one of them moreover for the occasion) to convey the meaning of our Greek word? Was there any necessity for it? Was there no single English word that would express the sense? There was *repentance,* the word adopted by the translators of the common English Bible. What objection lay to the use of that? Why was that passed by; and especially why was it passed by in order to give a preference to such a phrase as doing penance? If they had disliked repentance, they might with more propriety have employed the word *reformation.* It would seem as if they were anxious to avoid the use of any word which expressed or implied either *sorrow*

or *amendment,* and therefore they fixed on the phrase *doing penance.* I am mistaken if these translators have not a heavy account to give. This single rendering, if it were the only exceptionable one, would be as a millstone about the neck of that translation. Just think of the false impression, and that on a point of the highest moment, made on the minds of so many millions by this one egregiously erroneous version.

Contemplate the state of the case. God, in prospect of the judgment day, and by the terror of it, commands all men everywhere to do a certain thing, Acts 17:30-31; and Christ says that except they do it, they shall perish. Luke 13:3. This thing God expresses by the Greek term *metanoia.* But all do not understand Greek. Wherefore, for the admonition and instruction of those Catholics who read only the English language, and who cannot be persuaded of the sin of reading the Bible, it becomes necessary to render that word into English. Certain persons undertake to do it, that is, to interpret the mind of God as expressed by *metanoia.* And what do they make it out to mean? Hear, hear! *Doing penance!* That is it, they say. "Do the penance which your priest appoints, after you have made your confession to him, and that is all." It is no such thing. This is a misrepresentation of the Almighty. This is not the subject of the command and warning to which reference has been made. And to suppose that it is on account of this that angels rejoice, i.e., when a sinner does penance, is truly farcical. O what a translation! "There is joy in heaven over one sinner that does penance." Truly angels must be easily made to rejoice, if this be the case! How it sounds! How offensive to the very ear, and how much more to the enlightened judgment, is this rendering: "God commands all to do penance. Except ye do penance, ye shall all likewise perish. He is not willing that any should perish, but that all should *return to penance!"* Shocking! Away with such a translation from the earth. The *Douay* Bible is not God's Bible; for it *purposely* misrepresents him in a main point, viz: on the article of repentance. Here is a translation of *metanoia,* implying *no sorrow for sin, no change of mind* (which the word literally signifies), *nor any moral refor-mation;* but only the doing of certain external, and generally puerile, things prescribed by a priest; all which may be done without any internal exercise – without any emotion of any kind. The word, according to the Catholics, makes no requisi-tion on the *heart* whatever. And truly, a man may be a good Catholic without ever *feeling* anything, unless it be the bodily pain of self-inflicted penance. And everyone knows that *think-ing* is not necessary to constitute a good Catholic. Wherefore a man may be a good Catholic without either *thinking* or *feel-ing,* that is, without any exercise of either mind or heart. All that seems requisite is mechanical *action. Maelzel,* the con-structor of automatons, could almost make one. Is this unchari-table? It is *true,* and ought to be said. It ought to be known and proclaimed that the religion of the church of Rome *overlooks the reason, conscience, and heart of man*, addressing no ap-peal to them, and indeed making no use of them. Is it then the religion of the Holy Ghost? Is this the Christianity of Christ? It cannot be.

I ought perhaps to say that I find, in one place in the Douay Testament, the Greek *metanoeite* translated correctly, *repent*. It occurs in Mark 1:15. Whether it was done in a mo-ment of relenting, or through inadvertence, I cannot say. It was never repeated that I can find. Perhaps the translators had to do penance for presuming to render the word in that one case correctly.

Do you not see what a difference it makes to the priests, if you give it out that *repentance* is the requisition? Then a sinner will be saved if he repent, irrespective of the priest. The *great High* Priest that is passed into the heavens will see to the case of every true penitent. But if the requisition be *doing penance,* in that case, there being something necessary which the priest prescribes, he has the poor sinner completely in his power. It makes the salvation to depend on the act of the *little low* priest. Do you wonder that the priests insist on the translation *do penance,* and forbid the people to read in a

Bible which requires them to *repent?*

There is a precious note in the Douay connected with this subject, which may afford me a topic hereafter.

CHAPTER THIRTY-ONE
The Hardest Religion

Among the compliments which our brethren of the Church of Rome pay to their religion, this is one. They say it is the *hardest* religion – that no other religion requires so much of its votary. Hence they would have it inferred that theirs must be the divine and only true religion. The yoke being so hard, and the burden so heavy, they must of course be Christ's.

I shall examine this claim to the precedence in point of difficulty. And something I am prepared to concede to the Church of Rome on this score. There is a part of her *faith* which I acknowledge it is exceedingly hard to receive. It requires a powerful effort doubtless to believe the doctrine of transubstantiation, viz. that the bread and wine of the sacrament are changed into... what? The body and blood of Christ? Not that alone, but also into his *soul* and *divinity!* Yes, it is hard to *believe* it is so, when one *sees* it is not so, and *knows* it cannot be so. It is hard to disbelieve at will those long-tried and faithful servants, the senses; and especially that first of the five, the sight. There is difficulty in the Catholic religion truly. It puts a tremendous strain on the mind.

There is also her doctrine about the necessity of baptism to salvation, which some of us find it very hard to believe. One

reason of our difficulty is that that doctrine bears so hard upon
the heathen, and particularly on the immense multitude of
infants who everywhere die without baptism. According to the
doctrine of Rome, that baptism is indispensable to salvation,
they are all lost just for the want of a little water! Poor things,
they fare no better than the thief on the cross who died without baptism. They get no farther than Paradise the first day. It
is a hard religion. This doctrine is cruelly hard upon *children*;
as her doctrine that money, by the purchase of prayers and
masses, releases souls from purgatory, is hard upon the poor.

So much for the difficulty of her *faith*. But *all* of that is
not so hard; as for example, her doctrine of *indulgences*. It is
never hard to be *indulged*. There is no hardship, but very great
convenience for a delinquent sinner to have such a bank to
draw upon, as the accumulated merits of the saints in by-gone
ages, who did more than they needed for their own salvation,
having loved God with considerably more than "all the heart,
and soul, and strength, and mind!" *This* doctrine does not
make the Roman Catholic religion a hard one – neither does
the doctrine of *venial* sins. You know they hold that there are
some sins whose wages is not death. They are excusable –
mere peccadillos. *We* recognise no such sins. We think with
St. Paul, that "cursed is every one that continueth not in *all*
things which are written in the book of the law to do them."

But perhaps when the Catholics speak of their religion as
a hard one, they refer not so much to its faith as to its *practice*. It is what they have to *do* that is so hard. But why do they
speak of it as hard? It looks as if it was a task to them – as if
they do not find their sweetest and purest delight in it. It
would appear as if they did not esteem the service of God as
much their privilege as their duty. One would suppose, to hear
them talk, that the commandments of God are grievous. I am
truly sorry for them that Christ's yoke, which, he says, is easy,
they find to be so *galling* to them. We, Protestants, never
think of speaking of our religion as hard. "Wisdom's ways"
we find to be "pleasantness, and all her paths peace." Our language is: "O how love I thy law! How sweet are thy words un-

to my taste! yea, sweeter than honey to my mouth!" But it seems not to be so with Catholics. I have been struck with surprise to hear even the most devout of them speak of the requirements of their religion as things which they *must* comply with. "I must," is the language which they use in reference to almost everything of a religious kind that they do. I have thought with myself how it is possible that their hearts can be in their religion, if they esteem it such a hardship. How will heaven be able to make them happy, if the exercises and acts on earth, most akin to those of heaven, are so irksome that they engage in them only from sheer necessity?

But I must advert to some of the hard practices which the Catholic religion requires of her votaries. There is that practice of confessing to the priest. Is not that hard! Truly it is. I think I should find it hard to tell everything, even the most secret thoughts, to anybody called a priest. And then to have to perform whatever penance he might please to prescribe. Yes, it is hard – so hard, and so absurd too that God has never required it at our hands. He says to the sinner, come right to me with your broken heart, and make your confession to me, for he is "in Christ reconciling the world unto himself, not imputing their trespasses unto them."

Again, *fasting* is reckoned among the hard things of the Catholic religion – and indeed it is hard not to eat when one is hungry. But that is not their idea of fasting. Their idea of fasting is in accordance with what St. Paul says to Timothy in his prediction concerning them, an *"abstaining from meats,"* or "whatsoever is sold in the shambles." Now there is nothing so very hard in that restriction. He must be very difficult who cannot satisfy his appetite out of all the variety of the vegetable kingdom, when he has moreover the liberty of the entire fish market.

But there is one thing about the Catholic religion in view of which I suppose I must admit it to be the *hardest* religion. It belongs strictly neither to faith nor practice. You will guess that I have in my mind – *purgatory*. Now, as a doctrine, there are many things about it hard to be believed, as, for example, that material fire should be able to act on an immaterial spirit, and thereby purify it too. But hard as purgatory is to be *believed,* it is still harder to be *suffered.* Yes, it is hard, after having gone through the whole routine of the sacraments, and lived long a good Catholic, then to die, and go into an intense fire. It is so hard that I, for my part, prefer the religion of poor Lazarus, whom the angels took straight to heaven; and of the penitent malefactor, who spent a part of the day on which he died, in paradise. By the way, St. Paul could not have been thinking of purgatory when he said, "to me to die is *gain.* " But I forget that he lived before the time of the Catholic religion.

CHAPTER THIRTY-TWO
More About Penance

———◆◇◆———

Let us hear both sides. In my former article on this subject, I objected to the translation *doing penance,* in the Douay Bible. But have the Catholics nothing to say in justification of their rendering? I suppose that whatever they have to say is expressed in a certain note on Matthew 3:2. "Do penance, for the kingdom of heaven is at hand," is the edifying translation of the passage. Our attention is then directed to this note, *"agite pœnitentiam, metanoeite,"* which word, according to the use of the Scriptures and the holy fathers, does not only signify repentance and amendment of life, but also "punishing past sins by fasting and such like penitential exercises." This is the sage note.

Now here is an acknowledgment that the ideas of *repentance* and *amendment* are intended in the original word. Why then is a translation of it adopted, which excludes both repentance and amendment. If the original includes them, yet their translation does not. A man may do penance, and yet neither repent nor amend – neither be sorry nor better. These translators must have thought that repentance and amendment, though included in the original word, were of little importance, otherwise they would not have suppressed them in their translation. They must have judged them too insignificant to be taken notice of in their standard version! As for us Protestants, we think that *to be sorry* and *to reform* are very important parts of repentance.

But, besides repentance and amendment, they say the original word signifies "punishing past sins, by fasting," &c. This is their assertion. Where are their proofs? I would like to see some of them, for the dictionaries tell us another story. Well, they appeal to the Scriptures and the fathers, "according to the use of the Scriptures and the holy fathers." Here are two authorities, though of very unequal weight in my estimation. I wish these translators had said where the Scriptures use this word in their sense. I suppose they would, if they had been able. The truth is, the word is never so used. It does not include this idea of theirs. *Punishing!* Repentance don't mean punishing. *Punishing past sins!* This is no very eligible phrase. It is quite too figurative for an explanatory note. And punishing them, how? *By fasting.* How does fasting punish sin? I cannot see how any fasting punishes sin; but I am sure the Catholic fasting does not. Do you know what Catholics mean by fasting? Not abstaining from food. No, to be sure. But changing their kind of food. Only abstain from *meats,* according to the prediction, 1 Tim. 4:3, and you may eat what else you please. Fasting, according to the opinions held by Catholics in the region of country where I live, and I suppose it is so elsewhere, consists in reducing one's self down to the low diet of fish (after all their kinds), *eggs, oysters, terrapins,* with all manner of vegetables, and every variety of *desert!* That is fasting, because there is no butchers' meat eaten. You may eat what is sold anywhere else but in the shambles. Now I cannot see anything very *punitive* in *such* fasting. A man's sin must be exceedingly sensitive to feel the infliction of such abstinence. I do not believe that sin is to be *starved* out of the soul in this way.

It is well enough sometimes to try the value of an explanation upon a passage in which the thing explained occurs, as for example, "God now commandeth all men every where to punish their past sins by fasting and such like penitential exercises." How does that sound? Do you really think that it is what the Lord meant?

CHAPTER THIRTY-THREE
A Fast-Day Dinner

Some plain, honest people may be surprised at the heading of this article, because it implies a dinner of some sort on a day of fasting, whereas, according to their old-fashioned notions there should be no dinner at all on a fast day. And truly fasting did formerly imply *partial,* at least, if not *total* abstinence from food during the period of the fast. It was thought that eating to *the full* was incompatible with genuine fasting. Indeed it was considered that eating at all broke a fast. I suppose no one doubts that Daniel, Nehemiah, Ezra, and the pious Jews in general, abstained entirely from food on their days of fasting. Who has an idea that they ate any dinner on those days? But mind has marched a great way since those men flourished. Whether its march has always been *forward*, I leave others to determine. *Now,* according to the views which prevail in that church which cannot go wrong, and which does not make mistakes even when she contradicts herself, abstinence is not essential to a fast; and a fast-day dinner, so far from being no dinner at all, as some puritanical Christians still contend it should be, is a rare repast – one of the very best dinners in the whole week. I ought to say here that some Protestants have imbibed this doctrine of the infallible church, and very complacently practice according to it. We have a great many Pro-

143

testants among us who do not *protest* as thoroughly or as
strenuously as we think they should.

What put me in mind of this subject was the following
incident. As I was sitting at table the other day, the topic of
conversation was a very delicate preparation of eggs. I took
no particular interest in it, until one of the company remarked
that when she resided in the family of Mr. A., a distinguished
Catholic, that dish was always a part of their fast-day dinner.
This arrested my attention. Fast-day dinner, I exclaimed! Who
ever heard of a dinner on a fast-day?

It is not possible they have a dinner at Mr. A.'s on fast-
days! Dinner! replied the person. I never desire to eat a
better. This made me curious to enquire what constituted the
fast-day dinner at Mr. A.'s table. Well, said she, to begin, a
rock fish dressed with eggs and butter (no mean affair this
where there is an appetite), *eggs* prepared in two ways, and
oysters. They dispense with *vegetables* I presume, said I. O
no, she rejoined; and to this I readily assented, for I had for-
gotten myself in supposing that they dispensed with vegetables. Timothy does not prophecy of the Antichrist that he
shall command to abstain from vegetables, but only from
"meats, which God hath created to be received with thanksgiving." Well, surely, said I, they have no desert on their
fast-days? How you talk, said she; they have the very best,
and every variety. And do they call that a *fast-day* dinner?
and do they suppose that they fast when they eat it? Certainly, said she. Well, I suppose it is because they eat very
sparingly of what is set before them. You are mistaken, replied my informant, *quantity* has nothing to do in the matter.
It is not the quantity eaten that constitutes a fast, but the
kind. There the conversation ended, but my thoughts pro-
ceeded on. And this, thought I, is fasting. So the church
teaches, and millions on their way to the judgment believe it.
What dupes! how deceived to suppose that this is fasting. If
not deceived themselves, what insulters of God, to endeavor
to palm it off on him as fasting! A *change of food* is fasting!
To eat *differently* on one day from what we do on other days,

is to keep a fast! Admirable doctrine!

CHAPTER THIRTY-FOUR
The Mass

There is a great deal of the phraseology of the Romish church which is not a little peculiar, not to say *outlandish*. The Christian reader who is not very familiar with other authors than those who by inspiration wrote the Bible, does not know what to make of these terms when he comes across them in books professing to treat of Christianity. "The mass, the mass," he repeats to himself, "what is that?" He has read his Bible through and through, but he has found nothing about the mass there. He thinks it ought to be there, if it is any part of Christianity. Why should apostolical Christians have been silent on a subject on which those who claim to be their direct descendants are so loquacious? He does not even meet in his Bible with any doctrine or rite to which the word mass seems at all appropriate. He would not object to the word, if he could find the *thing* there. It never occurs to him that by the mass Catholics can mean the transaction recorded by Matthew in his 26th chapter, and by three other sacred writers, and which we commonly speak of as the institution of the Lord's Supper. But that is what they mean by it. Then, they tell us, the first mass was said. In the Douay Catechism we find these questions and answers: *Q.* Who said the first mass? *A.* Jesus Christ. *Q.* When did he say it? *A.* At his last supper. Here it is,

question and answer for it, if not *chapter and verse*. The biblical reader will please bear in mind whenever hereafter he
reads the narrative of the transaction, that the writer is giving
an account of the first mass that was ever said!

But they may call it mass, if they please, and they may
speak of Christ's instituting the ordinance as his saying mass.
Words are nothing, though it is certainly best that they should
be well chosen and fitly applied. If they mean by their mass
what we mean by the Lord's Supper, that is the main point.
But the truth is, they mean by it as different a thing as you can
well imagine. Just hear what the *Christian's Guide* says on
the subject: "I profess likewise, that in the *mass* there is offered to God a true, proper and propitiatory sacrifice for the
living and the dead." Christ offered it first when he said mass,
and every priest now offers it when he says mass. Well,
reader, you and I must not judge rashly. We will look again at
the account given of the matter in the Bible, and we will see
if we can find in it anything of the nature of a sacrifice. He
"took bread and blessed, and brake and gave it to the disciples, and said, Take, eat." And then he took the cup and gave
it. Where is any *sacrifice* here, and especially where is any
propitiatory sacrifice? Does the account we have of sacrifices
in the Old Testament, and in the epistle to the Hebrews, accord with what was done on this occasion? The Catholics say
that when Christ performed these actions with the bread and
wine, *he offered himself to God as a propitiatory sacrifice.*
How does what he did, bear even the least resemblance to the
offering of a propitiatory sacrifice? There was no bloodshed
– no life taken, as was the case in all propitiatory sacrifices
under the law, and in the sacrifice which Christ made of himself on the cross, and which has always, by Pagans, as well as
the disciples of the true religion, been considered as essential
to a *propitiatory* sacrifice. I confess there was *something* offered. Bread and wine were offered. These might constitute a
eucharistic sacrifice, but never a propitiatory one. If things of
this kind can constitute a propitiatory sacrifice, then I do not
see why Cain, who offered "of the fruit of the ground," was

not accepted equally with Abel who brought to the Lord "of
the firstlings of his flock." But whatever was offered, it was
not offered to God. A sacrifice, to be a sacrifice, must be offered to God, as even the quotation from the *Christian's
Guide* recognizes. But what was offered in this case was offered to the disciples. "Take, eat," he said to them. It is true
the bread and wine were offered them as the memorial of a
sacrifice in which the body of Christ was to be broken and his
blood shed; but the memorial of a sacrifice is not a sacrifice.
The emblematical representation of a thing is not the thing
itself. Plainly there was no sacrifice in this transaction.

But again: if Christ in the eucharist offered himself a sacrifice to God, as they affirm; and afterwards, as all admit,
offered himself on the cross, then he *twice* offered himself;
and if so, the writer of the epistle to the Hebrews was under
a great mistake, for he says, "Christ was once offered to bear
the sins of many," "we are sanctified through the offering of
the body of Jesus Christ *once for all.*" Heb. 9:28, and 10:10.
Here is a contradiction. Which shall we believe? The apostle
of the Gentiles or the Catholic church? If Christ really offered
himself in the eucharist – on the *table,* as Catholics contend
– there was no need of his offering himself on the *cross.* His
twice offering himself was quite unnecessary. If "in the mass
there is offered to God a true, proper, and propitiatory sacrifice," what need of another on Calvary? One "true, proper,
and propitiatory sacrifice" is all that is wanted.

But if the Catholic doctrine be true, Christ has been offered not twice only, but innumerable times. In every mass
that ever has been said, he has been offered. He is offered to-
day as really as he was on the day of his crucifixion. He is
offered on earth while he is interceding in heaven. Both parts
of the priest's office, the propitiation and the intercession, are
going on at the same time – a thing unheard of in the history
of the priesthood! Did the Jewish high priest, the type of Jesus, our great high priest, execute both parts of his office at
the same moment? Moreover, according to this doctrine, there

was no propriety in Christ's saying on the cross, "It is finished," for it is *not* finished yet, nor will it be, till the last mass is said. It depends on the will of the priest when it shall be finished. This to me is *shocking* doctrine. What! Can a priest cause Christ to be offered just when he pleases? My mind recoils from the conviction. There is what by a figure is called the "crucifying of the Son of God afresh," but this appears like doing it literally.

I know the Catholics make a distinction here. They say, and let them be heard, that Christ in the eucharist is offered in an *unbloody* manner, while the sacrifice of the cross was bloody. And this distinction they lay great stress on. But I wonder they see not the consequence of this explanation that if the sacrifice is unbloody, it cannot be propitiatory, which nevertheless, they say it is. Unbloody, yet propitiatory! Who ever heard of an unbloody propitiatory sacrifice? What Jew? What Pagan? A propitiatory sacrifice, be it remembered, is a sacrifice for atonement – a sacrifice with a view to the remission of sins. This all acknowledge. But "without shedding of blood is no remission," Heb. 9:22 – consequently no propitiatory sacrifice. Now here is no shedding of blood, they say; yet remission is effected by it! It is a *propitiatory* sacrifice, notwithstanding. Who does not see the contradiction? They must take back their admission that it is unbloody, or else acknowledge that it is not propitiatory. They cannot hold to both without self-contradiction.

The reader sees that this doctrine of the Catholic church subverts that great principle in the divine government, that "without shedding of blood is no remission" – a principle not merely inscribed on the pages of the Bible, but written with the finger of God on the mind of man. The conscience of the veriest pagan reads it there. If a sacrifice may be propitiatory, though unbloody, never a victim that bled under the Jewish economy, need have been slain; *and Christ need not have died!* The doctrine of the mass therefore, that a sacrifice may be propitiatory, though bloodless, undermines the Gospel.

One inference more from their doctrine I must not forget. It is this. If in the eucharist a propitiatory sacrifice is offered, then a propitiatory sacrifice may be effected by mere *action*. No passion whatever is necessary to it – expiation is made without any suffering – made by a mere *doing!* Is this truth? Can *antiquity* be pleaded for this doctrine? Can that be the *oldest* religion which cherishes and teaches it?

There is *no* sacrifice in what is improperly called the mass – least of all a *propitiatory* sacrifice. The doctrine is error – error in a capital particular – on a fundamental point – gross and most pernicious error. What then shall we think of a church which not only inculcates it, but gives it the greatest prominence, and makes the service connected with it the main thing in its religion? I have my thoughts. The reader must have his.

I reserve some things on the mass for a future communication.

CHAPTER THIRTY-FIVE
More About the Mass

⎯⎯⎯◈⎯⎯⎯

But before I proceed to the mass, I wish to add a word about *relics*. In my communication on that subject, I referred to Bellarmine as quoting from the Old Testament in support of the doctrine of relics. Since then, I have recollected a fact which makes me wonder that a Catholic should ever appeal to the Old Testament for authority in favor of relics. The reader probably knows that no relics are more common among the Catholics, and none more highly valued than the bones of deceased saints and martyrs. Now, if Numbers 19:16 be consulted, it will be found that under the Jewish dispensation, if a person so much as touched the bone of a man, he was ceremonially unclean for seven days, and had to submit to a tedious process of purification before he could be restored to the privileges of God's worship, from which he had been temporarily excluded in consequence of that contact. This being the case, it is pretty certain that the bones of the dead were not handled and cherished as relics by the pious Jews, as they are by our Catholics. There was nothing which the Israelite more carefully avoided than some of those very things which are now carried about and shown as relics. Therefore, I say, it is not best to go so far back as the Old Testament for testimony in favor of relics.

Now let us go to the mass again. It is known, I suppose, that they quote Scripture in favor of the mass. That circumstance however proves nothing. Scripture is not always aptly quoted. It should be remembered by those who are prone to think it in favor of a doctrine, that its abettors appeal to the Bible in its support, that Scripture was once quoted by a celebrated character to prove the propriety of the Son of God casting himself down from the pinnacle of the temple. It is always advisable to refer to the quotation, and see for ourselves if it makes in favor of the doctrine. The principal passage which the Catholics adduce in support of their mass, is that concerning Melchizedek, in the 14th chapter of Genesis. Abraham and his armed servants were on their return from "the slaughter of the kings," when they were met by this distinguished personage. The record of the occurrence is as follows: "And Melchizedek, king of Salem, brought forth bread and wine; and he was the priest of the Most High God. And he blessed him.... And he gave him tithes of all." Here is the text, reader. Now the doctrine deduced from it is this that "in the mass there is offered to God a true, proper, and propitiatory sacrifice for the living and the dead." Q.E.D.

Do not smile at the incongruity of the text and the doctrine – the distance of the conclusion from the premises. Sacred things are to be handled seriously. I know the reader only smiles at the *logic* of the thing. But he should remember that they do the best thing they can, when they quote this passage in favor of their mass. If there were other Scripture more appropriate and to the point than this, they would quote it. I have no doubt the intelligent Catholic is ashamed of this reference to the Bible in behalf of the mass. He sees that it has no bearing on the case. It is not to compare in point of appropriateness with the tempter's quotation referred to above.

Just observe *first,* that it was as *king,* not as priest, that Melchizedek brought forth the bread and wine. "Melchizedck, *king* of Salem, brought forth bread and wine." It was an act of royal bounty – an exercise of kingly hospitality. True, it is said

said immediately after, that he was a priest as well as a king; but that is said in reference to what follows, not what precedes. "And he was priest of the Most High God. And he blessed him." In his capacity of king, he brought forth bread and wine. In the exercise of his priestly office he blessed Abraham. To bless, we know, was one part of the priest's office. Numbers 6:23. His bringing forth bread and wine had nothing to do with his being a priest. What proves this view of the passage correct is, the manner in which the author of the Epistle to the Hebrews refers to it. In his *seventh* chapter he introduces Melchizedek as a priest. and in that character as the model of Christ's priesthood; and he speaks of his blessing Abraham, but says not a word about his bringing forth bread and wine. Why is not this circumstance – this most material circumstance, according to the Catholic notion – alluded to, if in it he acted as a priest and as the sacerdotal type of Christ? Why does the apostle, when speaking of him as a priest, mention only his benediction of Abraham? Now if, as I think it is manifest, he brought forth bread and wine not in the exercise of his office as priest, it overturns the Catholic argument at once.

But *secondly,* consider what in all human probability was the object of the bread and wine. Would anyone, in reading the passage, suppose it could have been for any other purpose than refreshment? What an idea! to come out to a people returning famished and weary from the toils of conflict, with a sacrifice – a propitiatory sacrifice too – the mass – with bread and wine, not to be eaten and drank, but to be offered to God! What more unnatural than such a supposition! On the other hand what more natural, and proper than to bring forth, for those fatigued soldiers, "wine that maketh glad the heart of man, and bread which strengtheneth man's heart," to refresh them? It was just what, under the circumstances, they needed.

In further proof of the correctness of this view of the passage, we find that Abraham recognized the priesthood of Melchizedek, not by receiving bread and wine at his hands, but by giving him tithes. "And he gave him tithes of all."

We see then there is no proof of any sacrifice in this transaction. There was nothing offered to God. What was offered, was to Abraham and his company. But if the offering was to God, it could but constitute an *eucharistic* sacrifice. Bread and wine might be offered as thank-offerings. But a bloodless propitiatory sacrifice was unknown under the Old Testament. Whatever view we take of the passage, it cannot make for the mass. That which was offered was only bread and wine. The Catholics do not pretend that they were changed into the body and blood of Christ. Melchizedek lived nearly 2,000 years before Christ had a body. How could transubstantiation take place so long before the incarnation? But if simple bread and wine were offered, then the act of Melchizedek, if anything more than an example of hospitality, was rather the model of the Protestants' Lord's Supper, than the Roman Catholic's mass. And here it may be observed, that Melchizedek does not seem to have denied the cup to the laity, as later priests have done. O no, it was the Council of Constance, in the 15th century, that established that custom.

But Catholics have another argument from Scripture in favor of their mass. It is derived from the perpetuity of Christ's priesthood. If, say they, Christ is a priest forever, and "every high priest is ordained to offer gifts and sacrifices," there must be a perpetual sacrifice, else he would be a priest without exercising priestly functions. But do they not see that this is to suppose Christ a priest after the order of Aaron, and not after that of Melchizedek? It is true the Aaronic priests offered sacrifice during the whole term of their priesthood. They stood "daily ministering, and offering oftentimes the same sacrifices." But what is said of Christ? He "needeth not daily, as those high priests, to offer up sacrifice, for this he did once, when he offered up himself." And again: "But this man, after he had offered one sacrifice for sins, forever sat down on the right hand of God." Yet the Catholics say he *needeth* daily to offer up sacrifice, and that he, as well as the Aaronic priests, offers oftentimes the same sacrifices! They

make Christ to resemble the Jewish priests in those very particulars in which the apostle says he stands in contrast to
them!

As to Christ's being a priest *forever,* if that means
anything more than is expressed in Heb. 7:24, where he is said
to have "an unchangeable priesthood," that is, a priesthood
that passes not from one to another, as did the Aaronic, it is
explained in the succeeding verse, where it is said that "he
ever liveth to make intercession." He is a priest forever,
because he ever liveth to make intercession. It is not at all
necessary that he should ever live to offer sacrifice, in order
to his being a priest forever. Intercession is as much a part of
the priest's office as sacrifice. And here I would ask whether
the Jewish high-priest was not as much a priest when he went
into the most holy place to sprinkle the blood of the sacrifice,
and to burn incense, as when, before he entered, he was
engaged in offering the sacrifice? Undoubtedly he was. He
offered no sacrifice while he was in the holy place. He went
in for another purpose altogether. So Christ, the great antitype, has entered "not into the holy places made with hands,
which are the figures of the true; but into heaven itself, now
to appear in the presence of God for us." And there he
remains. He has never come out. He had no need to come out
to offer another sacrifice, as the Jewish high-priest had. "By
one offering he hath perfected forever them that are sanctified." Were another sacrifice necessary, he would return in
person to earth to offer it; nor would it be "under the form of
bread and wine," for the apostle argues, in Heb. 9:25-26, that
he must suffer as often as he offers himself – that he cannot
be offered without suffering. Yet the Douay Catechism says
he "continues daily to offer himself." He is sacrificing,
according to them, while he is interceding – sacrificing in the
place appropriated to intercession, and offering himself
without suffering! The Bible tells us, "Christ was *once*
offered," but that "he *ever* liveth to make intercession." It
makes the perpetuity of his priesthood to consist in his
intercession. The Catholic doctrine, on the other hand, teaches

us that he is *continually* offered, and *therefore* a priest forever. And yet they appeal to the Bible in proof of their doctrine!

CHAPTER THIRTY-SIX
The Host

———◆———

Here is another of the *peculiar* terms of the Catholic religion. Protestants commonly use the word to signify an army, or a great multitude. But Catholics mean by it one thing. It is the name they give to the consecrated wafer in the Eucharist. Wafer! What has a wafer to do with the Eucharist? We read that our Saviour took *bread* and blessed, and break, and gave it to his disciples; but we read nothing about any wafer. If by wafer the same thing is meant, which we mean by bread, yet why this change of names? Why not call it what Christ called it? Why seek to improve upon things as they were left by him?

When the wafer, the thin piece of bread, is consecrated; that is, when a blessing has been invoked, and thanks have been given, for that is all that Christ did (the same precisely which he did when he fed the multitudes; in which case not even Catholics contend that there was any transubstantiation of the bread into another substance; and if no such effect was produced on that bread by the blessing and thanksgiving, how should the same produce such an effect on the bread of the sacrament?), then it is no longer called a wafer. It is true, St. Paul calls it the same afterwards that he called it before. But not so the Catholics. Now they call it the host, a word derived from the Latin *hostia,* signifying victim, or sacrifice.

But why change its name? And above all, why give it so different a name? One minute to call a thing a wafer, and the next a victim, a sacrifice! and when nothing but a prayer has intervened. Has it become so different a thing that it deserves so different a name? I know the Catholics say a great change has taken place in its nature, and therefore it ought to have a new name. Well, I am open to conviction. When a great change has taken place in anything, such a change that the original substance of the thing has totally departed, which is the greatest change anything can undergo, it commonly appears to the senses different from what it did before. But the wafer and the host *look* exactly alike, and they *smell* alike, and *taste* and *feel* precisely alike. The *form* is the same it was before; and by every test by which the *substance* can be examined, it is found to be the same. Yet they say the two things are as unlike as bread, and the body, soul and divinity of Christ! And this on pain of perdition must be believed, though the senses all exclaim against it; and reason, that calm faculty, almost getting into a passion with the absurdity of the doctrine, cries out against it; and though all experience be against it. And in favor of it, there is what? Why, Christ said, "This is my body," speaking as Paul did when he said, "and that rock *was* Christ;" and as he himself did, when he said, "I *am* the door." Did anyone ever contend that Christ was literally a *door* or a *rock*? Oh no. Why then is it contended that the bread was literally his body? Is it so said? And are not the other things also so said? It is strange the Catholics should contend for a literal interpretation in the first case, while they will not allow it in the other cases.

But if they contend for a strictly literal interpretation of "this is my body," why do they not abide by such an interpretation? Why do they say, as in the *Christian's Guide,* page 14, that "in the most holy sacrament of the Eucharist, there is truly, really, and substantially, the body and blood, *together with the soul and divinity* of our Lord Jesus Christ?" If Christ says it is his body, he does not say it is his soul and divinity. Where do they get that from? They say it is his body, because he says it is. But why do they say it is his soul and divinity also, when he does not say so? You see they do not interpret the passage literally, after all.

But what do the Catholics do with this host? Principally two things.

1. They *adore* it. The Bible says, "Thou shalt worship the Lord thy God, and him only shalt thou serve." But the Catholics worship the host. Yes, but is not Christ to be worshiped, and do they not hold that the host is Christ? Suppose they do hold so. Does it follow that everything is as they hold it to be? And if in this case the fact be different from what they hold it to be, is not their worship idolatry whatever they may verily think? Paul verily thought that he ought to do many things contrary to the name of Jesus of Nazareth. But did his verily thinking it was his duty, make it so, or exculpate him? No, he ought to have been better informed. And Catholics ought to be better informed than to suppose that the host is Christ – a wafer, God – a bit of bread, not only the body, but the very soul and divinity of Christ! I say they ought to know better. And if they do not, they must take the consequences of such ignorance!

2. The other thing which they do with the host is to *eat* it. This is all very well on our theory. It is bread; and what is bread for but to be eaten? Christ tells us to put it to this use. He says, "Take, eat." But on their supposition that it is bread no longer, it is no longer proper to be eaten. Its nature being so changed, there ought to be a corresponding change in its use. If it is to be adored, it is not to be devoured. Common sense teaches this. These two uses of it, adoring it and eating it, are incongruous to each other! One of them at least ought to be dispensed with. If they continue to eat it, they ought to give up adoring it. But if they must have it as an object of worship, they should cease to use it as an article of food. Anybody can tell you that you ought not to eat what you wor-

ship. *Cicero* thought such a thing could not be. In his work on Theology, he asks, "Was any man ever so mad as to take that which he feeds upon for a god?" But Cicero did not live late enough, else he could not have asked that question. Papal Rome has far outdone Pagan Rome.

If I believed in transubstantiation, I would never receive the Eucharist, I know that I must *spiritually* eat the flesh and drink the blood of Christ, that I may have life in me, that is, I must by meditation and faith, contemplate and appropriate his sacrifice; but I could never *literally* eat what I believed to be my divine Saviour. What, take him actually between my teeth! chew and swallow what I had just before worshiped, and adored! Let not the language be objected to. It is unavoidable. Rather let horror be felt at the thing. I would not speak lightly of sacred things, nor untenderly of the opinions of others; but the idea of adoring and eating the same object is shocking to me. Some readers will perhaps say that I must misrepresent the Catholics – that it is impossible they should believe so. Let such convict me of misrepresentation, if they can, and I will take the first opportunity of retracting.

CHAPTER THIRTY-SEVEN
Priests

———◆◇◆———

Where are we? Under what dispensation are we living? One would suppose, from hearing so much said among a certain class of people about *priests,* and their offering *sacrifice,* that the Old Testament dispensation – the dispensation of types and shadows – was still in force: and that the Messiah, the substance and antitype, was yet to come. Priests were a sacred order of men under the Jewish dispensation, and sacrifice constituted an important part of divine service. But, under the Christian dispensation, there is no order of priests, neither any literal sacrifices offered. We have, indeed, under this dispensation, a great High Priest, Jesus the Son of God, who, having once offered himself to bear the sins of many, has passed into the heavens for us, where he ever lives to make intercession; and he makes all his disciples, in a sense, both "kings and priests unto God" – Rev. 1:6; even as also *Peter,* who is prime authority with us all, testifies. When addressing the Christians to whom he wrote, he says: "Ye are a holy priesthood, to offer up spiritual sacrifices." 1 Pet. 2:5. This priesthood, which Peter recognizes, is very different from the Roman Catholic priesthood. All Christians share equally in the New Testament priesthood, and these priests are set apart to offer up *spiritual* sacrifices, or as it is said, v. 9, that they "should show forth the praises" of God. This is not the object of the Roman priesthood, neither are its functions performed by all the faithful.

The truth is, the Roman Catholic priesthood, that large and influential body of ecclesiastics, has no more warrant and authority for its existence from Christ, than it has from Mohammed. There is no more in the *Bible* in favor of such an order, than there is in the Koran, and perhaps not as much. Christ instituted no such office – authorized no such characters in his church. "He gave some, apostles; and some, prophets; and some, evangelists; and some, pastors and teachers;" but he gave none priests. And these he gave or appointed "for the perfecting of the saints. for the work of the ministry, for the edifying of the body of Christ," not for saying mass, offering sacrifice, burning incense, hearing confessions, and the like of those things. Christ appointed no officer to perform such functions as these. I have quoted from Eph. 4:11-12. In 1 Cor. 12:28, we have another enumeration of the officers which God has set in the church, but there is not a word about priests. They are a class of persons not at all needed under the Christian dispensation. The great High Priest of our profession answers every purpose. He has offered the sacrifice which is efficacious to put away sin – has shed a blood which cleanseth from all sin; and he ever liveth to be our Advocate with the Father. Neither for propitiation, nor for intercession, need we any other priest. Other priests are quite out of place since he has come.

If Christ instituted an order of priests, why do we not read anything about them in that choice piece of ecclesiastical history, the Acts of the Apostles? It is very strange. We read about Jewish priests in the Acts, and mention is made of the priests of Jupiter, but not a word do we hear of any Christian priests. Who were they? What were their names? Stephen was a deacon; Philip was an evangelist; Paul was an apostle; Peter was an elder, and there were many who were addressed as bishops. But who was a priest? If Paul was, why does he not sometimes call himself so in the introduction of his Epistles?

Was he ashamed of the office? Peter says he was an elder or presbyter, but gives no hint of his having been a priest. He seems to have had no idea of his being a priest in any other sense than as being one of that "holy priesthood, to offer up spiritual sacrifices," which all true believers compose.

If the priesthood be a Christian order of men, why does Paul, in writing to Timothy and Titus, take no notice of it? He gives the qualifications of bishops and deacons, but says nothing about those of priests. Were they to have no qualifications? Must a bishop be "blameless, the husband of one wife, vigilant, sober, apt to teach," &c. and might a priest be anything he pleased in these respects? Might anybody be a priest? If not, the silence of the apostle is decisive. Anyone may see now why the Catholic priests do not like the Bible. Who likes to be treated by book or man with *silent* contempt? The priests will never forgive the evangelists and apostles for having passed them by in the way they have done. Never. And they will never let their people have the genuine Bible. If they do, they will lose the people.

I suppose it is scarcely necessary to say, that if Catholics meant no more by a priest, than some of our Protestant brethren mean by the word, viz. a presbyter, of which priest, as used by them, is but an abbreviation, there could have been no occasion for this article. But they mean by a priest, a real *sacerdotal* character, as much as the priest of the Old Testament was – one who literally offers sacrifice. They pretend that their priests offer sacrifice now – that whenever they perform mass, a true, proper, and propitiatory sacrifice, for the living and the dead, is offered by them. And if you ask them what they offer, they tell you they offer Christ – that, under their hands, he becomes again, and as often as they choose to make him so, a propitiatory sacrifice – that he is as *really* offered by them in their missal service, as he was by himself on Calvary, only now he is offered in an unbloody manner! This is what their priests do. A priest must have something to offer. He is ordained to offer gifts and sacrifices. Now, the Catholic priest, finding nothing else to offer, pretends to reoffer Christ. For all this – this priesthood, and this sacrifice – everyone knows there is no more authority in the Bible than there is for the Hindoo Suttee – the burning of widows.

CHAPTER THIRTY-EIGHT
The Celibacy of the Clergy

———◆◈◆———

This is the Roman Catholic doctrine; but is it *Bible* doctrine? I believe, however, that the Catholics say it is no part of doctrine, but of *discipline*. This is a sorry evasion. It amounts to a confession that some of their ecclesiastical practices have no warrant in Christian doctrine. It is saying that it is a part of their discipline that their clergy *do* not marry, but no part of their doctrine that they *should* not.

But let us see how this doctrine or discipline, or by whatever name it may be called, tallies with the Scriptures; and as we proceed, we shall see why the Catholics are unwilling that the people should read the Bible. We shall see what a world of trouble it would occasion the priests, were they to be in the habit of reading it. Suppose, for example, an intelligent Catholic to take up Paul's *first* epistle to Timothy for perusal. Well, he reads along until he comes to the third chapter, where he finds Paul telling Timothy what a bishop must be. He must be this and that, and, among other things, "the husband of one wife." The reader is shocked. "Why, what does this mean? Our priests tell us that a bishop must not marry at all. Our church prohibits all her clergy from marrying. Which is right, our priests and church, or St. Paul?" He concludes to read on. Coming to verse 4th, he meets with this qualification of the bishop: "one that ruleth well his own house," i.e., *family*. But how can he, if not permitted to have a house of his own? He proceeds: "having his children in subjection." His *children* – his children!!! What, a bishop having children of his own, and having them collected in a family too! And then there follows a most provoking parenthesis, "for if a man know not how to rule his own house, how shall he take care of the church of God?" His ruling his own house well is to be a criterion of his ability to take care of the church of God, and yet they say that he must not marry!

But the apostle passes on to speak of the *deacons,* and to say what they must be; and in verse 11th, he says what sort of wives they should have – "even so must their wives be grave," &c. So far from encouraging a doubt whether they should marry or not, Paul gives them directions for choosing a wife.

Now, need anyone wonder that the priests do not want to have the Bible read by the people; a Bible which contains such statements as these, and which moreover declares that marriage is honorable in *all,* without exception of *clergy?* I do not wonder at it. Who would put into the hands of his children and servants, and recommend to their perusal and belief, a book containing statements so much at variance with his *oral* communications to them?

But there is a passage a little farther on, at the beginning of chapter 4, which, I suppose, constitutes with the priests a still stronger objection to the popular reading of this part of the Bible particularly: "The Spirit speaketh expressly, that in the latter times some shall depart from the faith – *forbidding to marry."* Now, they are afraid that if the people were to read this, they might say, "Why, St. Paul must mean our church; it forbids to marry." And as it might give the priests some trouble to show that he did not mean their church, the better way is not to let the people know that there is any such passage in the Bible.

CHAPTER THIRTY-NINE
A Holier State Than Matrimony?

In one of his last letters to Mr. Breckenridge, Mr. Hughes, of Philadelphia, says that the Catholic church does not forbid marriage, but "she holds, however, that there is a *holier state.*" When I had read the letter thus far, I stopped, and said to myself, "How is this? a holier state! I must look into this." So I thought a moment; and I came to the conclusion that I could not hold with the Catholic church in this thing, for the following reasons among others.

1. Because, according to this doctrine there is a holier state than that to which *Enoch* attained, and from which he was translated! He, we know, was a married man, and begat sons and daughters; and it would seem that he married *earlier* than any other Patriarch! And yet all the while after his marriage, for three hundred years, *he walked with God;* and "he had this testimony, that he pleased God;" and God, in honor of his eminent piety, translated him "that he should not see death!" Now do you suppose I am going to believe that the *state* of a Roman priest is *holier* than that of Enoch; and that he would have been a better man if he had let marriage alone? Never. I would ask, Do the priests do more than *walk with God?* Have they a higher testimony than that they please him? Are they *translated?* What is the reason we never hear of their

holier state being thus honored?

2. If there be a holier state than matrimony, why did not the law of the Jewish priesthood enjoin celibacy, as the letter tells us the law of the Catholic priesthood does? Above all, why was not the high priest, whose functions were of the most sacred character, so much as *permitted* to occupy that holier state? He was not only authorized, but, it is believed, was *obliged* to marry.

3. The letter says, speaking of the Catholic church, "the law of her priesthood enjoins celibacy, &.c. She does not choose them [those who marry] for her clergy." Truly, *she* is very *fastidious* in the choice of her clergy. Why need she be so much more *particular* than Paul required Timothy and Titus to be in the choice of their clergy? *Their* bishops and deacons might have a *wife;* but if any "wish to marry," *she does not choose them for her clergy!*

4. I thought when I read about *the holier state,* "What if all the world should aspire to the holier state?" Certainly, if it is holier, they ought to aspire to it. Priests are not the only persons who are commanded to be *perfect*.

Let the Catholic priesthood no longer make such an ado about their celibacy, as a *holier state*. Protestants allow their clergy to do as they please in this matter. If they remain unmarried, it is all very well. At the same time they are not extremely solicitous that their ministers should aspire to any holier state than that from which Enoch was translated.

CHAPTER FORTY
Auricular Confession

———◆◇◆———

I have been thinking with myself, where is the authority for this doctrine and practice of the Catholics – whence came the idea of confessing sin to a priest? Everyone admits that sin ought to be confessed – but why to a *priest?* Common sense would seem to dictate that confession should be made immediately to the being offended; especially if he be easily accessible. If a child offends his father, does he confess the offence to some *third* person, when his father is near at hand too; and above all, does he select for that third person, an equally offending brother? Was ever such a thing heard of as this? Yet this is the Catholic doctrine. It sends us to a brother as deep in the offence as we, to confess to him, that we have sinned against our father, when that father is nearby, and when, moreover, he says, "Come to me!" I think both the brothers, the penitent and the priest, had much better go directly to the father. I find that this is what they used to do in old times. I have been looking into the Bible to discover how it was then, and I perceive that they all went to God to make their confessions. They did not stop at the priest. There was David, and Daniel, and Ezra, and Nehemiah, and I know not how many more. They all went with their sin directly to God. Read that precious Psalm, the 51st. There is David before God. He confesses to the one he had offended. "Against thee," he says. And may we not use that Psalm? May we not go and say "against thee?" Must we turn aside to the priest? The *publican* did not. He went straight on to God. And the *prodigal* did not stop short of his father. Why should we? *Why should Catholics?*

I think the sinner should go on to God – and I do not like that Catholic doctrine because it stops him as he is going to God. The sinner is on his way to confess his sin to his Maker, and to implore of him pardoning mercy, and it says to him, "you need not go so far – the priest will hear you confess – he can forgive you." I like better the Protestant doctrine, which speeds and cheers the penitent on his way to God.

Nor can I see why we want more than one mediator between us and God. Why is not Christ enough? How admirably qualified he is for his work! With one nature that reaches up to God, and another that reaches down to man, how excellently fitted is he to mediate for us! Do we want another between us and Christ? O no. Let the priest please not put himself in the way. Jesus says, "Come unto me;" we want no human priest between us and our "great High Priest, that is passed into the heavens for us."

I may be very dull, but really I cannot see for my part what is the use of the priest; for surely he cannot forgive a sinner, unless he repents; and if he does repent, God forgives him, and then who cares whether the priest forgives him or not. If confession to the priest is intended to supersede confession to God, it is certainly a great mischief. If not so intended, it is useless, for our being forgiven depends on the nature of our confession to God, as penitent or otherwise.

But they allege in support of their doctrine, a verse of Scripture, "confess your faults one to another." I suppose the reason they allege this is, that it is the best they can find for their purpose. They must be hard pushed for authority, when they resort to that passage. "Confess your faults *one to another.*" This implies something *mutual*. If I confess to the priest, he must confess to me, for it says *one to another*. This puts priests and all on a level. There is nothing *auricular* in this. Certainly we ought to confess our faults one to another, and to "pray one for another," as the same apostle exhorts. But this is by no means the Catholic doctrine of confession. That is quite a different thing.

On the whole, it is my opinion that the world can dispense with this doctrine, and with the practice founded on it, as well as with anything which it has in use.

CHAPTER FORTY-ONE
A Mistake Corrected

In the chapter entitled "Auricular Confession," this writer stated, that in looking into the Bible he discovered that all the penitents mentioned therein went directly to God to make their confessions of sin, and not to the priests; and he spoke of David, Daniel, Ezra, and Nehemiah, as examples in point. He finds, however, that he was mistaken in saying that they all confessed to God instead of the priests. There is one exception, and he is willing that the Catholics should have the advantage of it. It is the case of *Judas Iscariot,* recorded in Matthew 27:3-4. He did not go to God with his confession. He went to the chief priests, and it was to them he said, "I have sinned, in that I have betrayed the innocent blood." Here, we must confess, is an example of confession to a priest. But it is the *only* one, I believe, in the Bible. Judas also brought *money* (thirty pieces of silver) to the priests; so that the Catholics have authority (such as it is) for that part of their practice. I am determined I will do the Catholics justice. They shall have the advantage of every particle of Scripture which really makes in their favor. It is well known that they need it.

But, poor man! He got nothing by going to the priests. It was their cruel and contemptuous treatment of him, as much as anything else, that determined him to go and hang himself.

175

How differently even Judas would have been treated, if he had gone with a broken heart to our great High Priest Jesus! Ah, he had better gone to him whom he betrayed, than to them to whom he betrayed him. I think I shall always go to him, notwithstanding the example of Judas.

CHAPTER FORTY-TWO
Purgatory

There are no worse reasoners than the Catholics, and I suppose the cause of this is that they are so little accustomed to reason. Men rarely do *well* what they are not used to do. The mind needs to be disciplined to thinking and reasoning, else it performs these operations but very indifferently. Hence, you hear so many persons say *therefore,* when nothing follows, or, at any rate, that does not follow which they suppose. Of this, the Catholics, not being in the habit of thinking and reasoning, their very religion prohibiting these operations, afford us some wonderful specimens. Between their premises and conclusion there is often so great a gulf, so deep and wide both, that I have wondered how they manage to get over it. Let us hear them on the subject of purgatory. They feel as if they would like to have a little Scripture for this dogma of theirs – a text or two; not for the satisfaction of the faithful (for to them it is sufficient that the church believes the doctrine), but to meet the heretics. But where shall they find in the Bible anything favorable to purgatory? The Bible speaks plainly enough of *two* places beyond the grave but it says nothing about a *third* place. It tells us of a *heaven* and a *hell,* but of an intermediate purgatory never a word. It is true that some hundreds of years afterwards certain writers speak of it as a Christian doctrine, but I want to know why the *older,* the inspired writers, say nothing about it. We read frequently in the Bible of being purged from sins, but most unfortunately for the Catholic doctrine, the purging is done *in this life,* not after death; and it is done, not by *fire,* as that doctrine asserts, but by *blood.* So that those passages in which *purging* occurs, do not help the Catholic cause. Then they look in the Bible for the word *fire;* and they read of the fire that is not quenched, and of everlasting fire, prepared for the devil and his angels. But this will not answer their purpose. This fire is everlasting, and for devils as well as wicked men. They never imagined a purgatory for devils. The fire of *their* purgatory is to be quenched.

But there is a passage having *fire* in it, which they adduce as to the point. It is 1 Cor. 3:15: "yet so as by fire." These are the premises in the grand argument; and the conclusion is purgatory, a place of temporary punishment by fire after this life. Q. E. D. Those letters were never more out of place. If there existed independent and irrefragable proof from another quarter of the doctrine of purgatory, in that case it might be innocently imagined that the apostle had in his mind some remote allusion to it in this chapter; but that this proverbial phrase, "saved, yet so as by fire," signifying, as used by writers both sacred and profane, *a narrow escape out of a great danger,* should be relied on as the principal support of the doctrine, is truly marvelous! I always thought that the fire of purgatory was to *purify men's souls;* but the fire here spoken of is to *try every man's work.* Besides, it is not said that the person shall be saved by fire, but *so as* by fire; that is, with the like difficulty with which a man in a burning house is saved from its conflagration. A good man, who, on the precious foundation of Jesus Christ, builds worthless materials, such as wood, hay, stubble, shall suffer the loss of his work, yet he himself shall be saved, though with great difficulty, *so as by fire.* So much for the *main pillar* of purgatory.

But they point us to Matthew 5:25-26: "Agree with thine adversary quickly, while thou art in the way with him; lest at any time the adversary deliver thee to the judge, and the judge deliver thee to the officer, and thou be cast into prison. Verily, I say unto thee, thou shalt by no means come out thence till thou hast paid the uttermost farthing." Now I would look the intelligent Catholic, who refers to this in proof of purgatory, in the face, and ask him if he is in earnest; if he can think that the doctrine of purgatory derives any support from that passage. What is it but a most excellent piece of advice in reference to the settlement of differences among men? But they say, "Does not Christ, in Matthew 12:32, speak of a sin which shall not be forgiven, neither in this world, neither in the world to come; and does not this imply that some sins may be forgiven in the world to come?" It implies no such thing. That form of expression is employed but to strengthen the denial. Besides, how can they be said to be forgiven, if they are purged away by fire?

Ah, but does not St. Peter say that Christ went and preached to the spirits in prison? Where were they but in purgatory? But were all the giant sinners before the flood in purgatory? If so, there may be some hope for us heretics. But why should Christ go to purgatory to *preach* to the spirits there? It is not by preaching, according to the Catholics, that souls are liberated from purgatory, but by *prayers and masses,* well paid for. And why should Christ select out the antediluvian sinners, and preach only to them? Indeed, I think the friends of purgatory had better give up that text and not attempt to support their dogma by *Scripture,* but be content with *tradition,* consoling themselves with the reflection that though nothing is *written* about it, yet it has been *handed* down.

As for us Protestants, we do not believe in *burning* out sin – in salvation by *fire.* We *protest* against it. We believe in the *washing* away of sin, and that by the blood of Jesus alone: "The blood of Jesus Christ, his son, cleanseth *us* from *all* sin." What is there left for fire to do? The spirits of the just made perfect ascribe no part of their salvation to fire. No. Their ascription is "unto him that loved us, and washed us from our sins in his own blood." How could souls just come up out of purgatory, where they have been hundreds, perhaps thousands of years, undergoing the purification of fire, unite in this song?

CHAPTER FORTY-THREE
More About Purgatory

What low and unworthy thoughts the Catholics must have of the work of Christ and of the efficacy of his blood, that they should believe that after he has done all he can for a soul, and his blood has exhausted its virtue on it, it has still to be subjected to the action of an intense flame, for no one knows how long, in order that the expiation of its sins may be complete, and its salvation perfected! What a doctrine! Why, according to this, Christ was premature in saying on the cross, "It is finished." It was not finished. The expiation of sin was only begun on Calvary. It is completed in purgatory! O God, I pray thee rid and deliver the mind of man from this dreadful delusion, so derogatory to thy dear Son, our blessed Savior; and so injurious to thee, for it represents thee, who delightest in mercy, as punishing after thou hast pardoned; as requiring satisfaction from men, after thou hast accepted for them the satisfaction of Christ!

Now I know the reason why Catholics are never happy in the prospect of death – why the dying votaries of that religion never exclaim, "O death where is thy sting? O grave where is thy victory?" It is because they are expecting to go to a place of fire. How can they be triumphant in the "certain fearful looking for of judgment and *fiery* indignation?" How can their

religion be other than what it is: a religion of fear and fore-
boding.

I have a few more things to say upon this subject; one of
them is this: If there was in the time of Christ and his apostles
such a place as purgatory, it must have been a place of little
note and of little *use* – of little note, for they say nothing
about it – and of little use, because we hear of no one going
there. Lazarus did not go there, neither did Dives – nor did the
thief who was saved from the cross – nor did Judas. Paul
speaks of those Christians who are *absent from the body, as
present with the Lord*. Is Christ in purgatory? Is it there that
believers go to be ever with him? But hark! a voice from
heaven! now we shall know how it is: "I heard a voice from
heaven," says St. John, "saying unto me, write, blessed are the
dead which die in the Lord from henceforth; yea, saith the
Spirit, that they may rest from their labors." They that die in
the Lord, *rest*. Then certainly they are not in purgatory.

If purgatory is full of souls, who are helped by the prayers
of the faithful on earth, as Catholics say, why, in the multitude
of their exhortations, do the sacred writers never so much as
give us a hint about praying for those poor suffering souls?
What a cruel oversight it was in them!

I *smile* sometimes when I look at this doctrine of
purgatory. But I repress the smile. Ludicrous as the doctrine
is, it is still more pernicious. What does it do, that is so bad?
Why, it turns away the attention of the soul from Christ. It
says the very opposite of "behold the Lamb of God, which
taketh away the sin of the world." And then it tells men that
they may not only live, but die wickedly, and yet entertain the
hope of salvation. It proclaims the possibility of a *post-mor-
tem* repentance and purification from sin. It emboldens men
to go out of the world in impenitence, assuring them that
though they do, yet prayers and masses offered for them after
death can save them. It denies that we are to be judged and
dealt with according to the deeds *done in the body;* whereas,
the Bible declares that according to these, we are to receive.

On the whole, for this doctrine of purgatory there is neither Scripture, nor reason, nor common sense. This, however, *may* be said of it. It is a *profitable* doctrine. Yes, a *capital speculation*. There is no doctrine which pays so well. You have heard of *Peter's pence*. Here his boasted successors get their pounds.

CHAPTER FORTY-FOUR
A Strange Thing

I read the other day in a Baltimore newspaper the following article:

"Obsequies. – This day the Prelates and Theologians of the Catholic Provincial Council, now in session in this city, together with several other priests, celebrated the solemn office for the repose of the souls of the Right Rev. Doctor Fenwick, of Cincinnati, and De Neker, of New Orleans. The Right Rev. Doctor Rosati celebrated the High Mass, attended by the proper officers. After the Gospel, the Right Rev. Doctor Purcell, Bishop of Cincinnati, ascended the pulpit and preached a funeral Oration; in which he ably portrayed, in accurate and pathetic language, the virtues and services of the deceased prelates, the former of whom fell a victim to the cholera, after years of laborious and successful exertions; the latter was taken away in the bloom of youth and in the midst of his labors by the yellow fever. After the Mass, Doctor Rosati performed the usual obsequies."

Having finished reading the article, I withdrew the paper from my eye and I said to myself, Where am I? I thought I was in the United States of America. But that cannot be. This can be no other than Spain, Portugal, or Italy. And what *century* is this? I always thought that I lived in the glorious *nineteenth*.

But I must have made a mistake of nine at the very least. This surely must be the *tenth* century; the darkest of the dark ages – *seculum tenebricosum,* as the church historians call it – the *midnight of time! this day* the Prelates – *in this city* – celebrated the solemn office for the *repose*, &c.

Just then it occurred to me that I might have read the paragraph incorrectly. So I resumed the paper; but still it read the same. Then I threw it down, and I sat and thought: Well now, this is a strange thing – an extraordinary piece of business – praying for the repose of deceased saints – and those, too, prelates of the only true church – and prelates eminent for their "virtues and services" – dead a year, or thereabouts, and yet not at *rest!* – and this by confession of their own church! What must become of the less renowned Catholics, if the very best of their bishops are tossing and burning in purgatory a year after having sacrificed their lives in the service of God and their fellow-creatures; and need solemn offices said for the repose of their souls? I always thought that rest to the soul ensued immediately on the exercise of faith. Paul says, "We which have believed, do enter into rest;" and Christ says, "Come unto me, and I will give you rest; take my yoke upon you and learn of me – and ye shall find rest unto your soul." I always supposed it meant that they should find the rest as soon as they came; and not after a long life, and a long purgatorial period subsequent to that. But above all, I had got the impression that, if never before, yet in the grave, good men find rest. I must have contracted that belief, I suppose, by reading what St. John says, "Blessed are the dead which die in the Lord *from henceforth:* yea, saith the Spirit, that they may rest," &c. or possibly I got it from that other passage, "There the wicked cease from troubling, and there the weary *are at rest."* But it seems I am wrong. Here are two bishops dead, yet not at rest! If what St. John says is true, here is a dilemma. Either those bishops did not die in the Lord, or they are at rest. Will the prelates say that they did not die in the Lord? I suspect not. Then they must believe that they are at rest. And if so, why celebrate the solemn office for their repose?

Hoping it may not be a *mortal* sin (if it be only *venial,* I will risk it), I would ask how the Catholics know that these bishops of theirs are not at rest? Who told them so? Where did they learn it? It seems to me a *slander* on those men. Bishop Fenwick enjoyed an enviable reputation for goodness. I have often heard him spoken of by Protestants in terms of high commendation; and the article quoted speaks of "the virtues and services" of both. And now, after they have been dead so long, to tell the world that they are not at rest, and that their repose must be prayed for! If Protestants had dared to suggest such a thing about them, we should never have heard the last of it.

But it seems not only a slander on those men, but also a *reflection* on Christ. How imperfectly, according to the Catholics, he must have done his work that even those esteemed his most devoted servants must lie, and toss, and burn, nobody knows how long, after death, before the efficacy of his atonement will allow of their being taken to heaven! And where is the fulfillment of his promise, "Come unto me and I will give you rest. Ye shall find rest to your souls"? According to the prelates, &c., these bishops have not found it yet.

I would *dare* ask another question. How is it that the priests and prelates can tell with so much accuracy how long a soul remains in purgatory before it is released? How do they know just when to stop praying? I will not insinuate that they pray as long as the money holds out, and no longer; for in the case of the bishops, I suppose they *freely* give their prayers. I could not help thinking, if they did go first to purgatory, yet they may not be there so long as this. A year is a long time to be in purgatory. Hours pass slowly away while one is burning. O, is this a part of Christianity? Can it be? What an unsatisfactory religion, which will not allow its most eminent examples, its most virtuous votaries, to have repose even in the grave! *Credat qui vult, non ego.*

CHAPTER FORTY-FIVE
Canonizing Saints

———◆≫◆———

I was a good deal struck the other day in reading, in a Baltimore paper, the following notice: "On Monday, the 17th of March, St. Patrick's day, a solemn High Mass will be sung in St. Patrick's church, Fell's Point, and the panegyric of the Saint will be delivered." It suggested some thoughts which I beg leave to communicate.

Why should the 17th of March be called St. Patrick's day? How is it his day more than yours or mine? What property had he in it more than others? He died on that day, it is true. But was he the only one that died on that day? Many thousands must have died on the same day. Does a man's dying on a particular day make it his? Ah, but he was a saint. How is that ascertained? Who saw his heart? I hope he was a good man, and a renewed person. But I think we ought to be cautious how we so positively pronounce our fellow creatures saints. Especially should Catholics, since even *Peter* himself, though, as they affirm, infallible, did not express himself so confidently, for he says in his first epistle, 5th chap, and 12th verse, of Silvanus, "a faithful brother unto you, *as I suppose.*" But what if he was a saint? Every real Christian is a saint. If anyone doubts this, let him consult any part of the New Testament. I trust there were many saints on earth at that time; and

189

I doubt not that other saints died on that day as well as Patrick. I object altogether to the day being called his. I have no idea that the 365th portion of every year belongs peculiarly to St. Patrick. I have no notion of this parceling out the year among the saints, and calling one day St. Patrick's, and another St. Cecilia's, and so on. At this rate we shall have the whole year appropriated to dead saints.

Ah, but you forget that Patrick was *canonized*. The church made him a saint, and appropriated that day to him. But I have not much opinion of these *canonized* saints – the saints of human manufacture. I like the *sanctified* ones better. Our Protestant saints are "God's workmanship, created in Christ Jesus." But granting the 17th of March to be St. Patrick's day, why is it *kept?* What have we to do with it, who live so long after? Patrick died in 493, and here in the 19th century they are keeping his day! I think it is time to have done grieving for the death of St. Patrick, now that he has been dead more than 1300 years, and especially when he died at the good old age of 120. Really, I think it is time that even the *Irish* Catholics had wiped up their tears for him. Tears! why, they do not keep the day in lamentation for him, but in *honor* and praise of him. High mass is to be sung, as it appears by the advertisement. Now singing expresses praise – and his *panegyric* is to be pronounced. It is wonderful what a disposition there is among the Catholics to multiply the objects of their religious honor. O that they were but satisfied to praise the Lord that made heaven and earth! But no – they must have *creatures* to do homage unto – angels; and saints of their own making; and above all, the blessed Virgin, "our heavenly mother," as some of them call her. It would really seem as if they had rather pay respect to any other being than God! They cannot be satisfied with the mediation of Jesus. They must have creatures to mediate and intercede for them. They are always doing things, and keeping days in honor of the saints. How much they talk about *tutelar saints* and *guardian angels*. It would appear as if they had rather be under the care of any other beings than God!

Now the idea of still eulogizing, panegyrizing, and praising, here in these United Stales, one St. Patrick, who died in Ireland in 493, how absurd! How is piety to be promoted by it, I should like to know!

By the way, what is *high* mass in distinction from *low* mass? They differ in several respects. Among the peculiarities of high mass, this, I believe, is one, that it is more *expensive* than low mass. If you want high mass said for a poor suffering soul in purgatory, you have to pay more than you do if you are content with low mass. And so it should be, for the high mass is worth more. Low mass scarcely makes an impression on a soul in purgatory. It is high mass that does the business effectually and expeditiously.

As for us Protestants, we have nothing to do with these masses. We do not find anything said about them in the Bible. The Catholic will pardon me, I hope, for alluding to the Bible. I am aware that it is no good authority with him, except now and then a verse (entirely misunderstood), such as that about the rock, which they say was *Peter,* on whom the church was built, according to them! Only think now, a man that denied the *founder* of Christianity three times with profane oaths, himself the *foundation* of the whole church! Nothing else for it to rest upon but Peter! But the beauty of it is that this foundation should have had a long series of *fundamental* successors, down to the present Pope! I always supposed that when a foundation is laid, there is an end of it and that all after belongs to the superstructure. But this is a digression. I was speaking of us Protestants, that we reject masses. And so we acknowledge no distinction of days, but *the Lord's day*. We keep no saint's days. We keep the Lord's day. It is almost the only day that some Catholics do not keep religiously! They are so busy with their saint's days, that they quite overlook the day which "the Lord hath made."

It strikes me that in giving this notice, the priests should have used an easier word than *panegyric*. I wonder how many of our Irish brethren know what it means. But "ignorance is the mother of devotion," you know, is one of their maxims. What multitudes of them said, on the 17th of March, "blessed St. Patrick." Probably many more than said, "Hallowed be thy name." And every day how much more respect is paid among them to the *mother* than to the *Son!* It is as clear as demonstration can make anything, that the Catholic religion is *idolatrous*. Men may say that it is a very *uncharitable* remark. But if anyone will dare to say it is an untrue remark, I am ready to meet him. Let us inquire *first,* what is truth. *Then* we will come to the question, what is *charity*. And we shall find that charity is something which "rejoices in the truth."

CHAPTER FORTY-SIX
General Lafayette Not at Rest

A few days since I observed the following notice, taken from the Charleston *Roman Catholic Miscellany*: "There will be an office and high mass in the Cathedral on Monday, 30th inst. (June), for the repose of the soul of General Lafayette." Also the following, taken from the *Catholic Herald*: "A solemn high mass will be sung on Tuesday next, the 20th inst. (July) at 10 o'clock, at the church of the Holy Trinity, corner of Sixth and Spruce, for the repose of the soul of the late Gen. Lafayette." The General died, it will be remembered, on the 20th of May. I did not know that he had been heard from since, any more than the rest of the dead. But the Charleston and Philadelphia editors seem to have had accounts of him up to as late a date as the 29th of July. Forty days after his death, according to the one account, and sixty-nine days according to the other, his soul was not at rest; and they give notice that measures are about to be taken to procure its repose. I don't know where they got it. They do not say through what channel the intelligence came. They are very positive, however, in regard to the fact. I have often been surprised at the confidence with which Catholics make assertions, implying a knowledge of the condition of souls beyond the grave. One would suppose they had a faculty, peculiar to themselves, of seeing into the

invisible world. With what positiveness they speak of this one
and that other as saints in glory, and even pray to them as such.
I have often thought that many of the prayers of Catholics
might be lost from the circumstance of the persons to whom
they are addressed not being in heaven.

We Protestants do not lose any prayer in that way. We do
not pray to any being who we are not certain is in heaven. We
speak with positiveness of the future condition of characters
and classes of men – the righteous and the wicked – believers
and unbelievers. The Bible does that. But we *do* not, we *dare*
not speak of the condition of individuals with the same confidence; and especially dare we not say of this or that person
that has died, that his soul is not at rest. We think it better to
be silent concerning the spirit that has returned to God who
gave it, and wait for the great day to disclose the decision of
the eternal mind on its case, and that especially if the person
seemed to die in impenitence. We would not usurp the place
and prerogative of judgment. What Protestant, even though
belonging to the class of Calvinists, as some of us do, would
intimate that the soul of such a man as Lafayette is not at rest?

But the Catholics are not so reserved. They pretend to
know not only who are saints in glory, but what souls are
suffering in the fire and restlessness of purgatory. They can
tell you the names of the persons. They have printed in two of
their papers, at least, that the *good* Lafayette, as our country-
men are wont to speak of him, has not gone to rest. His body
rests; but his soul, they tell us, has as yet found no repose. It
has not obtained admittance into that place where "the wicked
cease from troubling, and the weary are at rest." The General
lived a long time where the wicked cease *not* from troubling;
and much annoyance received he from them, in the course of
his patriotic and useful life; and many trials and fatigues he
underwent for liberty and the rights of man. Now it seems to
me the Catholics take a great deal on them, when they say that
his soul is still subject to the annoyances and disquiet which
were his lot on earth. Yet they do say so. They appoint a day,

a good while after his death, to sing high mass for the repose of his soul. Of course they must believe that up to that day his soul is not in repose, else why seek its repose? If the person who inserted these notices were living in the papal dominions, or under the influence of Prince Metternich, or the ex-king Charles, I should not wonder at their proclaiming his soul not at rest, for Lafayette was never a favorite at Rome, Vienna, or in the court of Charles X. He loved liberty too well for that. But that American Catholics, and, if the reader will not smile at the incongruity of the terms to each other, *republican Catholics,* should assert such a thing of him, I am a little surprised. I almost wonder that the people do not resent it as an insult to the old general. If a Protestant minister should say from the pulpit, or through the press, that Lafayette is not at rest, his church and his person would be hardly safe. But the Catholics do it with impunity. And let them. All the penalty I would have them suffer, is the contempt of every intelligent mind.

But why do the Catholics suppose that Lafayette is not at rest? Is it because none are at rest when they die? Is this their doctrine? A comfortable religion to be sure! According to this, how is it "gain to die?" Who would be "willing rather to be absent from the body?" Or how can it be said, "O death where is thy sting?" since *here* it is, and sting enough. But he who wrote Phil. 1, and 1 Cor. 15, and 2 Cor. 5 was not a Catholic. Or do they conclude Lafayette to be not at rest, because only saints find repose in death, and he was no saint? I wish all the saints of the church of Rome had been as good men as Lafayette. They have canonized worse men than he. I have never inquired curiously into the devotional character of the general, but I am possessed of no proof that he was not a Christian. Certainly, I find in his moral history no reason why they should be so positive that he is not at rest. They might have made the appointment conditional, I should think – mass to be said for the repose of his soul, provided it be not at rest. But they insert no condition. They are sure he is not at rest.

Well, if he is not at rest, how are their masses to give him repose? Does the Bible say that they have that efficacy? I must be excused for being so old-fashioned as to appeal to the Bible. That book, since it says nothing about masses, cannot be supposed to say anything of their *tranquilizing* tendency. I always forget that the Catholics have another source of information on religion besides the Bible. Tradition they call it. They mean by it the *talk* of inspired men, when they had no pen in their hands; which being heard, was reported, and so has come along down by word of mouth. But I, for my part, am satisfied with what they *wrote*.

We, Protestants, cannot join the Roman Catholics in their solemn office for Lafayette. We hope there is no *need* of praying for the repose of his soul; and we are certain there is no use in it. We prayed for him while he was *living*. We did not wait for him to be dead first. Now that his spirit has returned to God who gave it, and the Judge has passed upon it, we leave it there. By the way, how do the Catholics know when to stop praying for the repose of a soul? The Charleston Catholics had their mass for him on the 30th of June. But it seems it was of no avail, for the Philadelphia Catholics are called together to sing theirs on the 29th of July. How long is this thing to go on? I am writing on the 31st of July. Is he at rest now? Was the mass of the 29th inst. more efficacious than that of the 30th ult.? Perhaps the next news from New York will be that mass is to be performed there for the repose of the same soul some day in August. I hope the church is not *infallible* in regard to Lafayette, as in other matters. I should be sorry to think him all this time *not at rest*.

I remember an old Latin maxim, *"Nil de mortuis, nisi bonum"* (say nothing but good respecting the dead), which, it seems to me, the Catholics have disregarded in the case of Lafayette. It is certainly not saying any good of a dead man, to say that he is not at rest. And it is *cruel* to *sing* about it. The Philadelphia mass was *sung*. Is it kind to treat a suffering soul in purgatory with singing?

CHAPTER FORTY-SEVEN
Prayers For the Faithful Departed

———◆❖◆———

I have taken up again that little book, *The Christian's Guide to Heaven,* published, as the title page assures us, with the approbation of the most reverend Archbishop of Baltimore. Parts of it I have heretofore reviewed, but I have not exhausted its contents. I find on page 198 of my edition, the title of this article, "Prayers for the Faithful Departed." Faithful, said I to myself; and is it for the *faithful* dead that they pray? I was so ignorant as to suppose that it was for wicked Catholics, being dead, they were so good as to pray, I thought there was no need of praying for deceased *Christians* – for the *faithful* departed. I got the notion somewhere, that good people, when they die, go where there is "fullness of joy," and "pleasures forevermore." I may have imbibed it from St. Paul, who says that when such are "absent from the body," they are "present with the Lord;" or perhaps I caught it from St. John, who speaks of the dead that die in the Lord, as "blessed from henceforth," and as resting from their labors. It is more likely, however, that I got the idea from our Saviour, who says to the church in Smyrna, "Be thou faithful unto death, and I will give thee a crown of life." It was natural that I should take up the idea in reading this, that prayers for the faithful departed were needless, since he says, if they were faithful *unto* death they should receive a crown of life. We are all liable to mistakes, that is, unless we are *infallible*. It seems, according to the Catholics, who profess to know all about these matters, that the faithful don't get the crown of life by being faithful *unto* death. No, they must be faithful a good while after death, before they receive it. That which they get at death is very different from the crown of life. They are a long time absent from the body before they are present with the Lord. They don't go to heaven, or paradise. They go to purgatory. This is the Catholic's creed. It does not seem to agree altogether well with the Savior's promise to the Smyrneans. A simple man would suppose that fidelity unto death was immediately followed by the crown of life. But they that *cannot err* tell us otherwise.

Somehow or other this doctrine of the faithful going to purgatory after death, and needing to be prayed out of it, seems to have been always out of the mind of the apostle Paul, when he had his pen in his hand, or was dictating to the amanuensis. He speaks of it as *gain* to die; but surely, to exchange earth for purgatory is no gain. *Air,* however impure or sultry, is more agreeable than the element of *fire*, if the one immediately followed the other. He overlooked purgatory; otherwise I think he would not have had the desire to depart. Perhaps he thought he would fare as well as Lazarus, who made no stop in purgatory; or as the penitent thief, who could not have made a long one, since he was in paradise the same day he died. It has always appeared to me, that according to the Catholic system, this man, of all others, should have gone to purgatory. He never did any penance on earth – never bought an indulgence – he repented only a few minutes before he died; and yet he goes direct to paradise! Who then may not?

But do they not give us *chapter and verse* for praying for the dead? It must be confessed they do. Here it is: "It is a holy and wholesome thought to pray for the dead, that they may be loosened from their sins." 2 Macb. 12:46. This *looks* like Scripture, though it does not *sound* much like it. It passes for Scripture with the Catholics; but it is *Apocrypha*. It is no more holy Scripture than the Koran is. I know the Catholics contend that it is as good Scripture as any. But ask the Jews if it is Scripture. *"Unto them* were committed the oracles of God." Ask them if the books of Maccabees were committed to them. They tell you no. They were not even written in Hebrew. The New Testament abounds in quotations from the Old Testament Scriptures. I wonder some of the writers of the New Testament had not quoted Maccabees, if it had been Scripture. I would ask anyone who reads it, if it strikes the ear as Scripture. It certainly does not. Besides, it is not in all cases *good sense.* The verse quoted in favor of praying for the dead is not good sense. They speak of praying for the dead as a *holy thought,* and of prayer as having an efficacy to *loosen* them *from their sins.* Now any child can see this to be no part of Scripture.

But I hasten to the prayer. "A prayer for the suffering souls in purgatory." It is a curious prayer. I should like to quote the whole of it. But some specimens must suffice. Here is one petition: "Have mercy on those who suffer in purgatory. Look with compassion on the greatness of their torments; they are more keenly devoured by their ardent desire of being united to thee, than by the purging flames wherein they are plunged." Observe, here are *spirits* in *flames;* and they are *purging* flames. Fire may refine and purify certain metals, but how it should act in that way on *souls,* is beyond my comprehension. The suffering occasioned by fire is very horrible; but it seems that it is nothing compared with what they suffer from the love of God, or the "ardent desire of being united to him." I wonder, if they have such desires after God, that they are kept in that suffering state. I wonder he does not take them up to himself. Why should they suffer so, since Christ has suffered for them, and they are the faithful who believe on him? Did not Christ suffer enough? But the prayer proceeds: "With them I adore thy avenging justice." So it seems the faithful are the objects of God's avenging justice. I always thought that justice exacted its full demand of Christ. I don't know what the *Apocrypha* says about it, but holy Scripture informs me that God can now be *just,* and the justi-

fier of him which believeth in Jesus; and that if we confess
our sins, he is faithful and just to forgive them. Are not the
faithful pardoned; and how is pardon consistent with
vengeance?

The prayer goes on thus: "Remember, O Lord, thou art
their Father, and they are thy children. Forget the faults,
which, through the frailty of human nature, they have committed against thee." Then a little farther on: "Remember, O
Lord, that they are thy living members, thy faithful followers,
thy spouses." Here you see these sufferers are God's children;
and they are suffering for mere *faults,* which they fell into
through *frailty.* This seems hard. But they are not only God's
children; they are Christ's living members, his faithful followers, his spouses; and he died for them – and yet there they are
burning – pardoned, yet suffering punishment – interested in
the satisfaction of Christ, yet making satisfaction for themselves – paying over again the penalty which the Savior dis-
charged. And this is the Catholic gospel! Is it not "another
gospel?" And yet "not another." It is *no* gospel. *It is a contradiction of the good news.*

I quote but one more petition: "Deliver them, O most merciful God, from that place of darkness and torture, and call
them to a place of refreshment, light and peace." The reader
will remember that this prayer is for the *faithful.* It is they
who, having been "faithful unto death," go to a place of darkness and torture. There they *"rest* from their labors." I don't
know, for my part, what worse can befall *unbelievers* than
this. Truly, here is no great encouragement to believing. What
a consolitary doctrine this to break in the ear of a dying disciple! Fear not, be of good cheer, thou art but going to the place
of "darkness and torture." Can it be Jesus who says this to his
faithful followers? Can this be *Christian* doctrine? It certainly
is not well calculated to make dying easy. With such a prospect before them, I do not wonder that Catholics find it hard
to die – verily death has a sting, and the grave a victory, if the
Catholic doctrine of purgatory be true.

CHAPTER FORTY-EIGHT
An Improvement

I always hail improvements. I am always glad to see things taking a turn for the better, even though the improvement be slight. We must not despise the day of small things. Rome was not built in a day, nor will she be overthrown in a day. A system that it took centuries to introduce, cannot be expected to pass away all at once. Even if the improvement be only in phraseology, I rejoice in it, because words not only signify ideas, but sometimes generate them; so that from using right words, men not unfrequently pass to holding correct ideas on subjects.

The improvement to which I refer relates to phraseology merely. The case is this. It is the habit among the Catholics, some few months or so after a considerable character dies, to open the church and have a service for him. This has heretofore been announced thus: "High mass will be said or sung for the repose of the soul of such a one, at such a time" – not, the reader will understand, because the soul is at rest, but that it may be at rest. The service is not eucharistic, but supplicatory. This, I observed, was done in the case of a recent western bishop, and also in the case of Gen. Lafayette, who, some months after he had died, was discovered not to be at rest. Now, a short time ago the Archbishop of Baltimore died; and

201

weeks having passed away, the time came to take notice of his soul. Accordingly it was done. But I was struck with the alteration in the wording of the notice. It ran thus: "A funeral service will be performed in the cathedral for the late Most Rev. Archbishop Whitfield." This is certainly better than the old way of announcing it. To be sure, it sounds odd to talk of a funeral service for one who was regularly buried some months before. Protestants cannot readily understand it. But waiving this, why the change of phraseology? The best explanation I can give of it is this: The Catholics see that the public sense of the community, though sufficiently in their favor, will not tolerate a thing of this kind without a degree of restlessness, not a little annoying to them, and perhaps likely to be injurious to their concern. For see, that reasoning animal, man, who is naturally a logician, and can reason without ever having studied the rules of reasoning, argues something like this: Either the soul for which the mass is said is at rest, or it is not at rest. If it is at rest, it is preposterous to pray for its repose. It is asking that that may be done which has been done already. When a thing is done, to pray for it is superfluous. Then is the time to give thanks. If, on the other hand, the soul is not at rest, then common sense, which is no fool, asks why they put off the mass so long – why they did not begin to pray for the repose of the soul sooner. It was not kind in them. And common sense, which is also a great querist, inquires how they know the soul did not go immediately to rest; or if it did not, how they know it is not at rest weeks and months after. Common sense, not finding anything about it in the Bible, wants to know how the Catholics get the information. And so, through fear of the investigation of common sense, they change the phraseology of the notice. It is wise. Well may the authorities of the Roman Catholic church stand in need of common sense. I do not know any more formidable foe of error and imposition. I confidently look forward to the overthrow of the Catholic religion; and I expect a great deal of the work of its destruction will be done by common sense. I have not the dread, which some have, that this religion is going to overrun our country, and rise to dominion here. There is too much common sense abroad in the length and breadth of the land to allow of such a result. The people of the United States *will think,* and they have a notion that they have a right to think for themselves, without sending to Rome to know if they may. And they will ask questions on subjects, not omitting religion, and they will insist on having a satisfactory answer. The inhabitants of the old world may, if they please, believe on the *ipse dixit* of the Pope, but we of the new, before we yield our assent, require a "Thus saith the Lord," or a *"quod erat demonstrandum,"* or something of that nature. You can never get a majority here to believe in contradiction of the five senses. They will stick to it that a thing is what they see and feel and taste it to be – in other words, that bread is bread.

CHAPTER FORTY-NINE
The Duke of Brunswick's Fiftieth Reason

A certain Duke of Brunswick, having many years ago abjured Lutheranism, and become a Catholic, thought it necessary to apologize to the world for his change of religion. It needed an apology. So he wrote down *fifty reasons* to justify the course he had pursued, and had them printed in a little book, which is entitled *Fifty Reasons Why the Roman Catholic Religion Ought to Be Preferred to All Others.* This book the Catholics have free permission to read. O yes – they may read any book but the Bible. There is no objection to their reading books which contain *the thoughts of men;* but the book which contains *the thoughts of God* is interdicted! Men know how to express themselves. Men can write intelligibly. But...!!

Fifty reasons! The Duke must have been conscious, I suppose, that his reasons were *weak,* otherwise he would have been satisfied with a less number than fifty. Why does a man want fifty reasons for a thing when *one* good reason is sufficient? *I* have but one general reason for not being a Catholic, and I consider that enough. It is *that the Catholic religion is not the religion of the Bible.* It is not the religion which Matthew, Mark, Luke, John, Paul, James, Jude, and *Peter* wrote about, as anyone may see who will compare the Holy Scrip-

tures with the Council of Trent. But you see, the Duke, feeling
that he had not one *good* reason for turning Catholic, gives us
fifty *poor* ones; thinking to make up for the weakness of his
reasons by the number of them; and calculating that fifty poor
reasons would certainly be equivalent to one good one.

Fifty reasons! I shall not now inquire what the *forty-nine*
were. But what do you think the sapient Duke's *fiftieth* reason
was – his closing, crowning reason – that with which he
capped the climax – the reason which, having brought out, he
rested from very exhaustion, consequent on the amazing effort
of mind by which it was excogitated?

The fiftieth reason! I will give it to you in his own words,
which I quote from an edition of his reasons, published by one
of the very best Catholics in the land, so that there can be no
mistake about it. After going on about something else, he says,
"Besides that, the Catholics, to whom I spoke concerning my
salvation, assured me that, if I were to be damned for embracing the Catholic faith, they were ready to answer for me
at the Day of Judgment, and to take my damnation upon themselves; an assurance I could never extort from the ministers of
any sect, in case I should live and die in their religion. From
whence I inferred, the Roman Catholic faith was built on a
better foundation than any of those sects that have divided
from it." Prodigious! – and there he stops. I think it was time.

I do not know whether to make any comment on this
reason or not. Sometimes comment is unnecessary, and even
injurious. I wonder the Catholics are not ashamed of this
reason. Indeed, I suspect the intelligent ones among them do
blush for it, and wish the Duke had stopped at forty-nine.

But let us look at it a minute. It seems the Duke was won
over by the generosity of the Catholics. They agreed that if he
were to be damned for embracing their faith (they admit the
possibility that he might be; whereas, the Protestant ministers
whom he consulted were too well assured of the truth of their
religion to allow of the supposition), they would take his place,
and be damned for him. Now I wonder the Duke had not re-
flected – (but there are stupid Dukes – this was a nobleman,

but not one of nature's noblemen) – that those very Catholics, who made him this generous offer, if their faith was false, would have to be damned for themselves! That which should leave him without a title to heaven, would equally leave them without one. I wonder the Duke so readily believed that the substitution would be accepted. What if they were willing to suffer perdition in his place? The *Judge* might object to the arrangement. What ignorance and stupidity it manifests, to suppose that one may suffer in hell for another, just as one serves in the army for another! What an idea such persons must have of the nature of future punishment, to suppose that it is transferable! I should like to know how one man is to suffer *remorse* for another. And again, what an admirable exemplification of the spirit of Christianity, that one should consent, on any condition, to lie in hell, for ever, sinning and blaspheming God! I am sincerely glad that no Protestant minister could be found to give his consent to an eternity of enmity against God. But the Catholics whom the Duke consulted, they loved the Lord so that they were willing to sin against him for ever and ever, with ever-increasing malignity of opposition, for the sake of saving their noble proselyte! "FROM WHENCE I INFERRED," says the Duke (but you have no capitals large enough for this conclusion), "the Roman Catholic faith was built on a better foundation than any of those sects that have divided from it." Admirable dialectician! He must be *Aristotle* himself, by metempsychosis.

I think that those who wish to live and die Catholics, had better keep their eyes shut. It is the safer way. If they open them almost anywhere, they will be in danger.

CHAPTER FIFTY
The Duke's Seventh Reason

---✦---

The Duke's *fiftieth* reason has been the subject of an article. Each of his reasons might be made the subject of one, but that would be giving them too much consequence. I have selected the seventh for some remarks, because I have several times, in conversation with Catholics, heard it alleged, and some considerable stress laid on it. The drift of it is this: Protestants acknowledge that some Roman Catholics may be saved, but Catholics contend that no Protestants can be saved. Therefore it is better and safer to be a Catholic, than a Protestant! But, perhaps, I had better let his Serene Highness speak for himself. He says: "But what still confirmed me in my resolution of embracing the Roman Catholic faith was this, that the heretics themselves confess Roman Catholics may be saved, whereas, these maintain there is no salvation for such as are out of the Roman Catholic church." Let us examine this reasoning. Catholics *say* that there is no salvation out of their church, and therefore, by all means, we should belong to it. But does their saying so make it so? Is this very *charitable* doctrine of the Catholics of course *true?* Is it so very clear that none are saved but the *greatest bigots* – none saved but those who affirm, and are ready to swear that none others but themselves can be saved? Have Roman Catholics never affirmed anything but what was strictly true, so that from their uniform veracity and accuracy, we may infer that they must be correct in this statement? Let history answer that question. This is more than we claim even for Protestants. No salvation except for Catholics! Ah, and where is the chapter and verse for that? I don't think that even the Apocrapha can supply them. If subsequent Popes have taught the doctrine, he who is reckoned by Catholics to have been the first Pope, did not. It is rather unkind, perhaps, to quote Peter against his alleged successors, but a regard to truth compels me to do it. It is true, Peter once thought that a person must be an Israelite to be saved, just as our Catholics hold that a person must be a Catholic in order to be saved; but the case of *Cornelius* cured him of that prejudice. That led him to say as recorded, Acts 10:34-35, "Of a truth I perceive that God is no respecter of persons, but in every nation he that feareth him, and worketh righteousness, is accepted with him." This sounds a little different from the Duke's premises. It is a little unlike the language of later Popes. They have not taken their cue from Peter. Peter was a little of a Catholic at first, but he soon got rid of it.

Now, if what the Catholics say about there being no salvation out of their church, is not true – if there is no Scripture for it, but much against it – if even Peter controverts it, it certainly does not constitute a very good reason for being a Catholic. Suppose that Protestants should give out to the world that none but themselves can be saved, would that make Protestantism any better, or safer, or worthier of adoption? Would our religion be more entitled to reception, if we should publish that *Fenelon* was lost forever, and that *Pascal* was excluded from heaven, and *Masillon* too, just because they were not Protestants, but in communion with the Church of Rome? I think not. Nor can I think that the Roman Catholic religion is entitled to increased respect and veneration, because Catholics assert as an undoubted verity, that such men as *Locke, Newton, Leighton, Howard,* and many others are beyond all question, in hell, not even admitted to purgatory, because, forsooth, they were not Catholics.

But the Duke's inference is from a double premise. Not only do Catholics say no Protestant can be saved; but Protestants allow that Catholics may. If Protestants were to say that Catholics could not be saved, then they would be *even* with each other, and there could be no argument in the case. But since Protestants allow that others besides themselves may be saved, while Catholics deny it, therefore the Catholic religion is the safer. See what credit the Catholics give our declarations when they seem to work in their favor. They build a whole argument on one. Why do they not give us equal credence, when we declare that the probability of salvation among Protestants is much greater than among Catholics?

But what is it after all that Protestants allow? They allow that *some* Roman Catholics may be saved. They allow that the fact of a person's being externally related to the Catholic church does not of itself shut him out from salvation – that if he believes with his heart in the Lord Jesus, and truly repents of his sins, he will be saved, *though* a Catholic: and that the fact of his being a Catholic, though much against him, does not preclude the possibility of his being a genuine penitent and a true believer. This is the length and breadth of our admission. It admits, as everyone must see, not that there is salvation *by* the Catholic religion, but *in spite* of it, to some who professedly adhere to that religion. If a Catholic holds understandingly to the merit of good works, the insufficiency of Christ's sacrifice, the worship of creatures, or similar unscriptural doctrines, we do not see how he can be saved; but we believe many, called Catholics, reject these doctrines in fact, though not perhaps in word, and rely on Christ's atonement alone for salvation. Now if Catholics are so absurd as not to admit in our favor as much as we admit in theirs, we can't help it, and we don't care for it. It is just as they please. We shall not take back our admission for the sake of making proselytes to Protestantism – and if they can draw off any from us by their exclusive notions, they are welcome to them.

But I must call the reader's attention to the extent of the Duke's inference. He infers the perfect safety of the Catholic religion, because Protestants admit that some Catholics may be saved! But is that a safe spot of which this only can be said that some of the persons occupying it, may possibly escape? And is it madness to occupy any other spot? The Duke exclaims, "What a madness then were it, for any man not to go over to the Roman Catholics, who may be saved in the judgment of their adversaries: but to sort himself with these, who, according to Roman Catholics, are out of the way?" What a madness indeed, not to join a people who may not all be lost! O what a madness to continue to be Protestants, when Roman Catholics say that they are out of the way! What if they do *say* so? What if every *Jesuit* missionary has ever so constantly affirmed? I suppose a Jesuit can say what is not so, as well as anybody else. I suppose it is not naturally impossible for one being a Jesuit, I will not say to *lie,* but to *err.* He goes on like a very Aristotle. "Who would not advise a man to take the safest way when he is threatened with any evident danger?" Certainly noble Duke, the safest way; but not of course the way which some say is safest. There are a great many *safest ways,* if all which are said to be safest, are so. But his bigness proceeds: "And does not that way which two opposite parties approve of, promise greater security than another which one party only recommends, and which the other condemns?" But that is not so. The two parties do not approve of it. So far from it that the Protestant declares the Catholic way to be an exceedingly dangerous way, while his own way, though pronounced by the Catholic to be fatal, can claim the most respectable testimony that it is the true and safe way. Then comes an illustration, which like a great many other illustrations, is well constructed, but happens to be totally inapplicable to the case in hand, "Who, in fine, can doubt, but that a medicine prescribed by two physicians may be taken with more security than another which one of the two judges may be his death?" How the Duke rolls on his argument! Just now the Protestant only admitted the *possibility* of the Catholic's salvation. Then he is represented as *approving* the Catholic way – and immediately after as *prescribing it!* It is easy proving anything, if one may make facts to suit his purpose. I believe it is not true that Protestants *prescribe* the Catholic religion to those who ask them what they shall do to be saved.

People must become Catholics, if they please, but I would advise them to look out for better reasons for the change than the Duke of Brunswick's fifty and especially than this, his seventh. It is a poor reason for becoming a Catholic that they say they are the people, and haughtily bid all others stand by, because they are holier. I cannot think it so great a recommendation of a religion, that it *denounces,* and so far as it can, *damns* all who cannot see their way clear to embrace it.

CHAPTER FIFTY-ONE
The Duke's Eleventh Reason

———◆◇◆———

I don't know what is to become of our Protestant religion, with so many reasons against it. I don't know but we shall all have to go back again to the Catholic church, compelled by the cogency of argument. *Fifty* reasons why the Roman Catholic religion ought to be preferred to all others! Only think. And some of them, that I don't find any answer to in any Protestant writer! Such a one is the *eleventh* of the formidable series. In the preceding reasons or considerations, as he calls them, the Duke had been giving us the result of his inquiries. It seems he was quite an investigator. He *searched* almost every book but the Scriptures. He looked for what he wanted everywhere but where the thing was. When a man is inquiring after the truth, and consults the philosophers, the fathers, the martyrs, and all the saints, I cannot see where is the harm of just looking into the prophets, the evangelists, and the apostles too. I don't know why they should be treated with such neglect; I think they are quite as respectable writers as some of the fathers. But be this as it may, the Duke, in his *eighth* consideration, tells us about his consulting the writings of the ancient fathers, to find what they would advise him to do, whether to embrace the Roman Catholic faith or no. And he says they all told him to be a Roman Catholic by all means.

Then says he in his ninth consideration, "I appealed to the saints of God, and asked them what was the faith they lived in, and by which they arrived at eternal bliss." And they said, not that they had "washed their robes and made them white in the blood of the Lamb," in accordance with the account given of some other saints in Rev. 7, but "they all made answer, it was the Roman faith." By the way, the Catholics have an advantage over us Protestants. They know just who are saints and have a way of consulting them after they are dead. *We* are not equal to those things. Why, the Duke even tells us the names of those who made answer. "Thus," says he, "I was answered by St. Martin, St. Nicholas, St. Athanasius, and many more among the bishops; among the religious, by St. Dominick (!?) St. Francis, &c. Among the widows, by St. Monica, St. Bridget, St. Elizabeth, &c. Among the virgins, by St. Agatha, St. Lucy, St. Agnes, St. Catharine, &c." I think if a Protestant had had the privilege of cross-examining the above when the Duke consulted them, the result might have been somewhat different. But no Protestant had notice of his intention to carry his inquiries into that quarter. The Duke was determined to make thorough work of it. Therefore, in his *tenth* consideration he tells us: "Then I turned to the holy martyrs, and inquired what faith it was for the truth of which they spilt their blood." They answered it was the Roman Catholic. "This," he says, "I was assured of by thirty-three bishops of Rome, who were crowned with martyrdom; by the saints Cyprian, Sebastian, Laurence; by St. Agatha, St. Cecily, St. Dorothy, St. Barbara, and an *infinite* number of other saints." They all told the same story. "Then," says the Duke, "I *wound up* my argument." But he concluded on the whole, before winding it up, to let it *run down* a little lower. And this brings us to his *eleventh* reason. The reader will please prepare himself now for a *prostrating* argument. "My next step was in thought to hell, where I found in condemnation to everlasting torments, Simon Magus, Novatus Vigilantius, Pelagius, Nestorius, Macedonius, Marcion, &c." May I never be under the necessity of descending so low for an argument!

But the Duke does not say that he *actually* went to the bad place, but he went *in thought*. There, having gone *in thought*, he found so and so. Here is another advantage the Catholics have over us. They know who are in hell. We do not. Perhaps some are not there whom we may fear are. We do not hold ourselves qualified to judge in these matters. Well, he found them there. He was quite sure not one of them had repented and been saved. And he asked them how they came there, and they very civilly answered that "it was for their breaking off from the Roman Catholic church." Now this is the argument that I have not seen answered by any Protestant writer, as far as I can recollect. I don't read of any Protestant who went even in thought to hell to consult the lost on the points in controversy between us and the Catholics. So that the Catholics have the whole of this argument to themselves. The Duke says they told him they were there for not being Catholics, and we have no counter testimony. Protestantism, however, having so many other "witnesses on the truth" of her system, can easily do without the testimony of "the spirits in prison." Let that be for the Catholics. But by the way, I wonder that the Duke relied so unhesitatingly on the testimony of those persons. How does he know they told the truth? Are not all such called in Scripture "the children of the devil," and does not everybody know his character for veracity? It is certainly an extraordinary answer for one of them, Simon Magus, to give, considering the time when he lived. How could he say with truth that he was there for breaking off from the *Roman* Catholic church, when at the date of his apostasy the Gospel had never been preached at *Rome?* There was no Roman church to break off from.

I was expecting that the Duke would push his inquiries yet one step farther, and, seeing he was on the spot, interrogate Satan in regard to the true religion. But he does not seem to have consulted "the father of lying," but only the children. The truth is, the Devil does not wait to be consulted on that subject, but makes his suggestions to "them that dwell on the earth," without being called on so to do.

I hope the Reformed religion will be able to stand the shock of this argument, notwithstanding the doubt I expressed in the beginning.

CHAPTER FIFTY-TWO
Beauties of the Leopold Reports

I have been not a little interested with the extracts recently published from the Reports of the Leopold Society in Austria, and it has struck me that I might do some service, especially to those who have not the time or the patience to read long articles, by calling the attention of the public to the *choice* parts of the reports; for even where all is good, you know, there are generally portions here and there of *superior excellence*. Will you allow me, then, to point out some of the *beauties* of the reports? What has struck me with peculiar force, will probably affect others as forcibly.

Now I have *admired* the way in which the report speaks of *conversions*. It seems that these Catholics can *foresee* conversions with as much certainty as we, poor blind Protestants, can *look back* on them! *F. Baraga* writes, under date of March 10, 1832: "I long for the arrival of spring, when I shall have numerous conversions!!" Now, I am aware that the *face of nature* is renewed when spring appears, but I did not know this was as true of the *souls of men*. It is news to me that conversions can be foreseen with such perfect accuracy. It is hard to foresee what men will do. But here is a foreseeing of what God will do, unless they deny that conversion is his work! But what makes our Catholic brother speak so confidently of the conversions that were to take place? How did he know it? Why, forsooth, some had promised him that they would be converted in the spring. "There are many pagan Indians," he says, "who promised me last summer and fall, that they would in the spring embrace the Christian religion!" This beats all. Why, if they were convinced of the truth of the Christian religion, did they not embrace it at once? Why put it off till after the 1st of March? Not only had some promised him on their honor that they would be converted, but he says: "From two other counties I have received assurances, that many of the Indians there would be converted to the Christian religion, if I would come and preach the gospel to them!" You see they had told others, who told Baraga, that they would. It came very *straight*. He speaks particularly of a *Christian* Indian who had brought him the intelligence. Now observe, they had never heard a word of the gospel – neither knew what it was, nor how confirmed! Yet they promised to embrace it – promised to believe, and be converted – to have their hearts changed – to be born again! I know that God promises, "A new heart will I give you," but I never knew before that any man, and especially one who had never heard the gospel, could look ahead and say, "At such a time I will have a new heart." Baraga says, "I cannot describe the joy such assurances give me." We Protestants are not so easily made happy by the promises of the unconverted.

Again, I have been struck with the manner in which Baraga speaks of the mother of Jesus, under date of July 1, 1832: "When I decided to be a missionary," he says, "I promised *our heavenly mother* that I would consecrate to her the first church I should consecrate among the Indians, for I am convinced she will pray her Son continually for the progress of our missions." *Our heavenly mother!!* "Our heavenly Father" is a phrase dear to every Christian heart; but it is the first time I ever heard we had a heavenly mother. O! O! Will the reader pause a moment and inquire the meaning of the word *idolatry?* Baraga *promised* her? Where had they the interview when that promise was made? He must have been praying to her. And why was the promise made? Because, "I am convinced she will pray her Son." What! *prayer* in heaven! John, in Patmos, heard *praise* in heaven, but not prayer. I know there is one advocate in heaven. Jesus Christ the righteous, who ever liveth to make intercession. That one is enough. But here we are told of another advocate on high – a mediatrix. And she prays *to* her son and mediates between him and sinners. What! Do we need a mediator between us and Christ? I always knew we needed a mediator between God and us; but I supposed we need go directly and immediately to Christ, since he is himself a mediator. Baraga says presently after, "Thanks be to Mary, gracious mother, who ever prays for the conversion of the heathen." Now, if all this is not idolatry, I wish somebody could tell me what idolatry is. I would as soon undertake to defend the worship of the *golden calf* as this.

Finally, what power these Catholic priests have! Protestant ministers are only "mighty through God." But the priests can succeed without that help. Father Senderl writes: "Young people of sixteen years, and not unfrequently older persons, have never confessed nor communed; [taken the *half sacrament,* I suppose he means.] *I* prepare them for both, and for confirmation." *I* prepare them! And another writes concerning Baraga, that he *achieves wonders of salvation* among the Ottawas.

This is a specimen of the religion which Prince *Metternich & Co.* our Austrian brethren, those dear lovers of liberty, are benevolently contributing to give us here in America. They are afraid that our *free institutions* will not be permanent unless they help us to prop them up with the Catholic religion! *Timeo Metternich et dona ferentem.* [I fear Metternich, even sending gifts.]

CHAPTER FIFTY-THREE
Puerility of the Catholic Religion

————◆≫◇≪◆————

What a *puerile* religion the Catholic religion is! How *childish!* How petty its cares! About what trifles it concerns itself! The Christian is truly "the highest style of man," but the consistent Catholic is not much above the *lowest*. Baraga writes as follows: "It would be of *essential* service to our missions, if there could be sent us cups, boxes for the holy wafer, rosaries, crucifixes – of the last two, as many as possible, for such articles cannot be bought here. How it is with church furniture and linen, you may easily think. Those given to me by pious persons are of great use to me, and I cannot be *thankful enough* for them." Cannot be thankful enough for boxes, rosaries, &c.!! His capacity for gratitude must be small indeed. We Protestants often feel that we cannot be *thankful enough,* but it is not for such *trumpery* as cups and boxes. When we feel and lament over the inadequacy of our gratitude, it is in view of the many and great mercies of God to us. I suppose our Protestant missionaries at Ceylon, and elsewhere, would not be so very grateful if we should send them a consignment of cups, boxes, &c. No: such things could not be of *essential service* to their missions. We do not understand converting people as the Catholics do. They can *regenerate* and *pardon,* and do all the rest in a trice. We have to bring before the *mind* of the sinner the great-saving truth of Christ *crucified;* but they have only to put the little *crucifix* in his *hand.* I went, a short time ago, to visit a man under sentence of death, to talk to him about Christ and his death. I found him gazing intently on a little metallic image of Christ crucified, which a priest had left him. He seemed indifferent to all I said. The priest had *prepared* him!

In a note to Baraga's letter, we are told of a great number of Catholic *notions* that are already on their way to America; among them three thousand *rosaries!* What a sight of *beads!* How their missions must prosper after this! A little afterwards, by way of inducing others to contribute beads, boxes, &c. it is said: "The good Christian rejoices to promote the external honor of the house of God, so that the inner man, by the splendor of the external divine worship, may be lifted to heaven." What a sage sentiment! How *scriptural!* How *philosophical* too! This is truly a new way of being lifted to heaven.

But I must not overlook a letter of Bishop Fenwick, dated *Mackinac,* July 1, 1831. He writes: "On the second day after my arrival, Mr. M. and I preached at different times after mass. When the people had heard some sermons, confessions began; and from that time till the day of our departure, we sat on the *confession stool* from early morning till 1 o'clock, and in the afternoon, from 3 or 4 o'clock, till 10, 11, and twice till 12 at night. There were confessions of twenty, thirty, and forty years." What a prodigious memory they must have had, who called to mind and confessed the sins of forty years! All that time they were waiting for a priest to come along. There was the God who delighted in mercy, to whom they might have confessed, as the publican dared to do; and there was "Jesus, the mediator of the new covenant," whom they might at any time have engaged to intercede for them. But that would not have been to act the part of good Catholics. The good Catholic docs not go to the *mercy-seat of God* to confess his sins and obtain forgiveness (that were an "iniquity to be punished by the judges"), but he waits for the priest to come along with his *confession-stool.* The confession-stool substituted in the place of the *mercy-seat!* This is one of the *doings* of that religion which Austria wants to give us. God says to sinners, "Come unto me," and he promises that he will "abundantly pardon them from his throne of grace." "Nay," says the priest, "Wait till I come with my little stool." Catholics may, if they please, go for pardon and mercy to the *stool of confession* – but, my Protestant brethren, "Let us come boldly unto the *throne of grace,* that we may obtain mercy, and find grace to help in time of need."

CHAPTER FIFTY-FOUR
Partiality of the Church of Rome

———◈———

There is nothing of which I am more perfectly certain than that the religion of the church of Rome is not the religion of Jesus Christ. I do not care to say what it is – but it is not Christianity. How can they be the same, when they differ so widely? Midnight and noon are not more unlike. I will specify one point of difference. Romanism is *partial*. She is a respecter of persons. Christianity is the very opposite of this. And not only is the church of Rome partial, but her partialities are all in favor of the rich. Now Christianity, if it leans in any direction, inclines towards the poor. It was one sign that the Messiah was come in the person of Jesus of Nazareth, that "the poor had the Gospel preached to them." They were not overlooked; far from it. "Hearken," says one, "hath not God chosen the poor of this world, rich in faith, and heirs of the kingdom which he has promised to them that love him." The poor had never such a friend as Christ. He was himself poor. He had experience of the privations, cares, and sorrows of that condition. So poor was he that he had not where to lay his head. No lodging-place at night had he in all that world which his word created and his hand sustained. The poor are peculiarly his brethren.

And think you, then, that he has opened a wider door of entrance into heaven to the rich than to the poor? Think you that he has connected with the condition of the rich man an advantage whereby he may sooner or more easily obtain admittance into the place of his glorious presence? I do not believe it. But this is what the church of Rome teaches. She preaches better tidings to the rich than to the poor – Christ did not. But I must make good this charge against the church of Rome. I do it thus: According to her creed, all souls, except, perhaps, now and then one, of every condition, go, on their leaving the body, to purgatory. There they are. Now to get them out. How does she say that is to be done? Why, they must either suffer out their time (that is, all the time which remains after subtracting all the indulgences that were purchased and paid for), or their release must be effected by the efficacy of prayers and masses said for them by the faithful on earth. You remember that mass was performed lately by the Catholic congress assembled in Baltimore, for the repose of the souls of two deceased bishops. There is no other way. Christ's sacrifice does not give rest to the soul, according to the Catholics, unless the sacrifice of the mass be added to it! Well, how are these masses, so necessary to the repose and release of the soul, to be had? Why, how do you suppose, but by *paying for them!* Give the priests money, and they will say them. At any rate, they promise that they will. Now, do you not see the advantage which money gives a man in the church of Rome, and the hardships of being a poor Catholic? I wonder any poor man should think the Catholic religion the religion of Christ. Verily, Popery is no religion for poverty. What did our Savior mean, when he said, "How hardly shall they that have riches enter into the kingdom of God?" According to the Catholic doctrine, they are the very men that enter most easily – they having the wherewith to purchase indulgences and masses. It is the poor, according to this scheme, that with difficulty enter in. They have to serve their time out in purgatory – whereas, the rich can buy their time off.

But is the thing managed in this way? Are not masses said for all that die in the Catholic faith? Yes, there is a day in the year called All-soul's day (it comes on the 2d of November.

Alas for the poor Catholic who dies on the 3d, for he has to
wait a whole year for a mass), when all of them are prayed
for. The poor share in the benefit of the masses said on that
day; but what does it amount to, when you consider the millions of Catholics that die every year, and the many millions
not yet out of the fire, among whom the benefit is to be divided? It is not like having a mass said for one's soul in particular. But that is the privilege of the rich.

Now I do not believe that it is the religion of the blessed
Jesus that makes this distinction in favor of the rich. I believe
that Christ brought good news from heaven to the poor as to
the rich. I believe that every blessing which he has to dispose
of may be bought *without money and without price*. See Isa.
55:1. I believe that "whosoever will," may "take of the water
of life freely." Rev. 22:17. This is my creed.

There was poor Lazarus. I reckon he went to heaven as
soon after he died as he would have done if he had had millions of money to leave to the church; and I reckon the angels
were as tender and careful of his soul as if he had been
clothed in purple and fared sumptuously every day. And he
was a poor man to whom the dying Savior said, "To-day shalt
thou be with me in paradise." If there was ever a man who,
according to the Catholic doctrine, should have gone to purgatory, and remained a great while there, it was that thief. But
you see he did not go there. Christ took him with him immediately to paradise. He went there without *penance,* without
extreme unction, without *confession to a priest,* without a
single mass being said for him, in utter outrage of all the rules
of the church! I don't think that Joseph of Arimathea, rich as
he was, could have got to heaven sooner than that penitent
thief. But Christ always considered the poor; and that is not
Christianity which does not consider them.

As I said in former pieces that I had no faith in salvation
by fire, or in salvation by oil, I say now I have no faith in salvation by *money*.

I will close with a syllogism. Christianity makes it as easy for a poor man to get to heaven, as for one that is rich. This is my *major* proposition. Who dare dispute it? But the church of Rome makes it not so easy for a poor man to get to heaven as one that is rich. This is my *minor* proposition, and this I have shown. Who dare deny it? Now my *conclusion* is, therefore, the religion of the church of Rome is not Christianity.

CHAPTER FIFTY-FIVE
Supererogation

———◆◈◆———

This long word was coined by the Catholics for their own special use, as was also that longer and harder word *transubstantiation*. Nobody else finds any occasion for it. It expresses what the rest of mankind think has no real existence. If the reader is acquainted with the *Latin* (that language which the church of Rome extols so highly above the Hebrew and Greek, the languages of God's choice – and in which she says we ought all to say our prayers, whether we know it or not), he will see that supererogation is compounded of two words, and signifies literally *above what is required*. It designates that *overwork* in the service of God which certain good Catholics in all ages are supposed to have done. After doing all the good which God requires of them, then what they do *over and above* that, they call *supererogation*. It expresses how much more they love God than they are required to love him. He claims, you know, to be loved with all the heart, and soul, and strength, and mind. This is the first and great command. And observe, it is with *all* of each. Now, when the Catholic has fully satisfied this claim, he enters upon the work of supererogation; and all that he does in the way of loving God after loving him with *all the four,* heart, strength, soul, and mind, is set down to this account, be it more or less. Might I just ask here, for information, if a man is required to love God with *all his strength,* that is, with his *whole ability,* how can he do more? It seems that whatever he can do, is required to be done. How Catholics contrive to do more than they can, I, for my part, do not know. It is a mystery to Protestants. We are in the dark on this subject.

Let me tell you more about this supererogation. It expresses how much more Catholics are than *perfect.* Perfect, you know, we are all required to be – perfect, "even as our Father who is in heaven is perfect." Matt. 5:48. And in another place, even by *Peter* it is said, "As he which has called you is holy, so be ye holy in all manner of conversation." Now, when one is holy as he who hath called him is holy, and holy in all manner of conversation, in so far as he is more holy than this, since this is all that is *required,* the surplus is set down to the account of supererogation! In other words, supererogation expresses the superfluous glory which men give to God, after glorifying him in their bodies and spirits, which are his, and doing *all* whatsoever they do, even to the matter of eating and drinking, to his glory! See 1 Cor. 6:27, and Acts 10:31. This is supererogation. I hope the reader understands it.

Now, those who do these works of supererogation, have of course more merit than they have any occasion for on their own account; and as this excess of merit ought by no means to be lost, the church of Rome has with great economy treasured it up for the benefit of those who are so unfortunate as to do less than what is required, to whom it is, at the discretion of the church, and for value received, served out in the way of *indulgences.* This is the article that Tetzel was dealing in so largely and lucratively, when one Martin Luther started up in opposition to the traffic. Protestants have never dealt in the article of indulgences.

By the way, the wise virgins of whom we read in Matthew 25, seem not to have been acquainted with this doctrine of supererogation; for when the foolish virgins, in the lack of oil, applied to them for a seasonable supply, they answered, "Not so: lest there be not enough for us and you." They had only enough for themselves.

But, say the Catholics, are there not *counsels* in the Bible, as well as *precepts* – certain things which are *recommended, though not required?* If so, and a person, besides obeying the precepts, complies with the counsels, doing not only what is required, but also what is recommended, is not here a foundation for works of supererogation? This is plausible, but that is all. My motto being *brevity,* I shall not attempt an extended answer to it, but take these few things.

1. If there are counsels recommending things which no precepts require, yet obedience to these counsels cannot constitute works of supererogation, and accumulate merit, unless all the *precepts* are perfectly obeyed. A man must do all that is required, before he can do more than what is required. Now, has any mere man since the fall perfectly obeyed all the commandments of God? Has any man done *all* his duty? If not, I reckon no one has done *more* than his duty. We don't generally go beyond a thing until after we have come up to it. A cup does not usually run over before it is full. But,

2. According to this doctrine of the church of Rome, men are capable of a higher virtue than God has required! They can, and actually do, perform virtuous and holy acts which belong to neither of the tables of the law, and which are comprehended neither in the love of God nor in the love of man! Is this idea admissible? The Psalmist says, "Thy commandment is exceeding broad." But according to this doctrine, the virtue of the Catholic is *broader.* I, however, don't believe it.

3. There is no counsel which does not become a precept or command, provided it be found that God can be more glorified by a compliance with it than otherwise. The thing recommended, if in any case it be apparent that the doing of it will redound to the glory of God, is *ipso facto* required, and becomes a duty. Take the favorite example of the Catholics – celibacy, which, they say, is recommended but not required. Now, if anyone find that he can better serve God in the single

condition than in the matrimonial state, celibacy is in that case his duty; and being a duty a thing required, it can be no work of supererogation. When celibacy is not a duty, there is no virtue in it. Does anyone believe that Enoch would have been more virtuous, and walked more closely with God, if he had not fallen into the mistake of matrimony?

But I arrest my remarks, lest, in criminating one kind of supererogation, I myself be guilty of another.

CHAPTER FIFTY-SIX
Convents

———◆◇◆———

Everybody knows how important convents, monasteries, nunneries, &c., are in the Roman Catholic religion. Who has not heard of monks and nuns, and of the establishments in which they respectively seclude themselves from the *world?* What a pity they cannot keep the flesh and the devil as far off! But the flesh they must carry in with them; and the devil is at no loss to find an entrance. There are no convents that can shut these out; and it is my opinion that it is not of much use to exclude the world, if they cannot at the same time shut out the other two. The world would be very harmless, but for the flesh and the devil. Besides, I am of opinion that a person may be *of* the world, though not *in* the world. *In,* but not *of* the world, is the Protestant doctrine, and the true plan. People forget that the world is not the great globe, with all its land and water; but that it is often an insidious little thing, which, ere one knows it, has taken up its lodgment in the heart. The heart can entertain the world. If so, convents cannot even keep out the world. They do not answer the purpose therefore for which they are intended.

But be this as it may, I find nothing for convents in the Bible. In the Old Testament not a word about them – in the New not a word. Now if they are such grand contrivances for making people good, and for keeping them pure, I am surprised they were never thought of till after the canon of Scripture was closed. Why do not the men who speak by inspiration of God say anything about them? This puzzles me. I wish some of the Catholic writers would explain the reason. They tell us why St. Paul omitted to say anything in his writings about the mass. It was, say the authors of the Rhemish Testament in their annotations on Hebrews 7:17, "because of the depth of the mystery, and the incredulity or feebleness of those to whom he wrote." We thank them for the admission that the apostle did not teach the doctrine of the mass. But how came they to know the reason of his silence upon it? May be it was for a similar reason that he maintained a perfect silence on the subject of convents!

But if convents are such clever things, why did not *Enoch* take the vow of celibacy, and go into one, instead of "walking with God and begetting sons and daughters?" How much better a man, according to the Catholic notion, he would have been, had he only been a monk! And why did not St. John banish himself to some solitary Patmos, and there live the life of a hermit, before a persecuting emperor drove him into it? Why did not *Peter* and his wife part, and he turn friar and she nun? We look to such characters for examples. Why did not the Marys, or some other of the pious women of whom we read in the Bible, take the veil? Monachism, they may say, is an improvement on those times. But I do not like the idea of improvements on a system arranged by the wisdom of the Son of God himself.

There is what we call the *spirit* of a book. Now, the entire system of convents seems to me as clearly at variance with the spirit of the Bible, as one thing can be at variance with another. The Bible appears to have been written for persons who were to live in society with their fellow-men. It supposes human beings to be associated together in families and in civil communities, not as immured in monasteries and shut up in nunneries. It takes up the various relations of life, and descants on the duties growing out of them. But the system of Monachism dissolves these relations. Is it scriptural then? But why should I ask if that be scriptural which was first instituted by St. Anthony in the fourth century after Christ?

Again, if the system is favorable to holiness, then all equally need it, since all are required to be equally holy – to be holy as God is holy. But what would soon become of us all, if the system should become universal, and all adopt these means of holiness? This idea, that the means of the most eminent sanctity required of any, are not accessible and practicable to all, is radically erroneous. It is no such thing. It cannot be. Therefore I conclude against convents.

But while I impugn the system, I bring no charges against the existing edifices, called convents. I would never have them assailed by any other force than that which belongs to an argument. If I were a Roman Catholic, I could not more indignantly reprobate than, being a Protestant, I do, the recent burning of one of these buildings. If truth and argument can prostrate them, let them fall; but not by axes, and hammers, and fire-brands. All I contend for is, that the whole concern of convents is unscriptural. Those who inhabit them may be as pure as any who live outside; and so I shall believe them to be, until I have proof to the contrary. This plan of suspecting, and of making mere suspicion the ground of condemnation, is no part of my religion. It is a part of my Protestantism to protest against it.

CHAPTER FIFTY-SEVEN
Mr. Berrington and Mrs. More

In reading the interesting memoirs of Mrs. Hannah More, I was struck with a letter which that good lady received in 1809 from Joseph Berrington, the Pope's Vicar General, taking exception to something she had said in her "Cœlebs in Search of a Wife" about Popery. He is very much offended with her. He complains, among other things, of her use of the word Popery, to designate the Roman Catholic religion. Now, some of us do not make much use of that word, as knowing it is offensive to the Catholics, and not willing to say anything irritating to them; and when we do use it, I believe it is more for brevity than for any other reason – to avoid tedious circumlocution. It is as much out of regard to the printer as anything else. I do not see, however, why they should so strongly object to the word Popery. They all hold to the spiritual supremacy of the Pope, and regard him as the head of the church. Why then should not their religious system be called after him? We call ours after the one we regard as supreme in spiritual matters, and head of the church. We call it Christianity, after Christ. Why not for the same reason call theirs Popery, after the Pope? We do not even get angry when they call us Calvinists, and our doctrinal system Calvinism. Yet with much more reason might we; for what is Calvin to us? He is only one of many thousand eminent men who have espoused substantially the system of doctrine we do.

I find in Mr. B's. letter this remarkable sentence: "Nothing is more surprising than that you Protestants should be so utterly ignorant, as you really are, or seem to be, of our tenets; when we all, whatever be our country, think alike, and our catechisms and books of instruction lie open before the world." He says nothing is more surprising. But there is one thing which is even more surprising. It is that any intelligent ecclesiastic should venture to write such a sentence. He says we Protestants are, or seem to be, utterly ignorant of their tenets. Now, the truth is, there are few things we are better acquainted with than the tenets of Roman Catholics. They say we do not let them speak for themselves. Yes, we do. Do they not speak for themselves in their own manuals, breviaries, and catechisms printed under their own sanction and supervision? If we take their tenets from their own books, and quote verbatim, and refer to the edition and page, is not that enough? Well, we do so. Yet they say we misrepresent them. How can that be? They may misrepresent and contradict themselves, but it is hard to hold us responsible for that. If we are ignorant of their *tenets,* it is because they do not themselves constantly *hold* to them. If they *let go* their doctrines, as soon as Protestants attack and expose them, and resorting to explanations, evasions and glosses, do thus virtually *take hold* of something different from their original and published tenets, we are not to blame for that, I should think.

But Mr. B. tells us what makes our ignorance so surprising: "when we all, whatever be our country, think alike." Do they all think alike? They did not always all think alike. See history. And so far as they do think alike, does the reader know how it comes about? It is by virtue of not thinking at all. But grant they all think alike. Does it follow that they think right? Has no error ever been very popular? The world all thought alike once on astronomy – all held the earth to be the centre of the system. But did they think right? However, it is convenient to have a large number of persons all think alike, for then, if you can ascertain what one thinks, you know what all think, and if you read one book, you know what is in them all. So, if you chance to fall in with a Spanish or Italian Catholic, and he tells you what he thinks, you know what every English and American Catholic thinks, for they "all think alike." So, if you take up one catechism or book of instruction and read that, you know what they all ought to contain. It saves a great deal of trouble.

But the Vicar complains bitterly of the Bishop of Durham, for asserting that the Catholics suppress the second commandment. He says it is no such thing, and that any school boy could tell him different. And he affirms that a catechism was put into the hands of the Bishop containing that commandment, and still he persisted in his assertion. The Bishop was right; and "nothing is more surprising" than that Mr. B should deny it. I have myself seen two different catechisms, published in Ireland by Catholic book-sellers, and under the highest Catholic authority, from both of which the second commandment was excluded; and it is left out of the *Christian's Guide,* published in Baltimore by the Catholics, as anyone may see for himself. Now what could Mr. B. say to this? Would he say, "O! those were published in Ireland and America"? But he says, "we all, *whatever be our country,* think alike." Would he say that he spoke of 1809, and these were published since? But it is their boast that they not only do now all think alike, but that they always did think alike. Would he say that if it was left out of those catechisms, yet it was retained in others? Yes; but if their catechisms differ, how do they all think alike? Besides, no one ever accused the Catholics of leaving the second commandment out of every one of their books. But why do they leave it out of any? Will they please to say why they leave it out of any? They have never condescended to answer that question. They always evade it. If a man should publish successive editions of the laws of any country, and should leave out of some of the editions a certain important law, would it be sufficient for him to say that he did not leave it out of all the editions? Why did he leave it out of any? Why did he not make them all uniform? A man may as well tell me I have no eyes, as deny that some Catholic catechisms have been published without the second commandment. Now, why was ever a catechism published under Catholic sanction without it? Did they ever publish one in which they omitted any other of the commandments? Did Protestants ever publish a list of the commandments with one omitted, and another divided so as to make out the ten? Alas for them! there is no getting out of this dilemma into which they have brought themselves by their mutilation of the decalogue. It is about the most unfortunate thing they ever did for themselves. I do not wonder that Mr. B. was restless under the charge. But surely, he had too much good sense to suppose that he had answered the Bishop, when he showed him a catechism that had the commandment in it. It is as if a man, charged with falsehood in a particular instance, should undertake to answer the charge by showing that in another instance he had spoken the truth. The Catholics are very uneasy to get rid of this millstone about the neck of their religion. They see it is in danger of sinking it. But they cannot slip it off so easy; and if they cannot manage to swim with it, it must sink them. Well, if it does, and nothing but the system goes to the bottom, I shall not be sorry.

In the course of his letter, Mr. B. speaks of "the *anarchical* principle of private judgment." And is this a principle which leads to anarchy? *Paul* did not seem to think so. He says: "Let every man be fully persuaded in his own mind." What anarchy must have existed in the Berean church, where, after hearing the word, they "searched the Scriptures daily, whether these things were so"! What confusion there must have been where all read and thought for themselves! They needed an Inquisitor to set things right. He is the man to mend matters when people fall to "searching the Scriptures." Well, if the 19th century will tolerate the denunciation of private judgment on any subject, I suppose it must be so; but I cannot say Amen.

CHAPTER FIFTY-EIGHT
A New Method of Exciting Devotion

There seems to be no end to new discoveries. Marching mind appears to have no idea of halting. Probably improvements will go on until the world itself terminates. What should I see, in taking up the *Observer* of January 3d, but an article headed "Cathedral at St. Louis?" Then followed a description taken, be it known, not from any scandalous Protestant paper, but from the *Catholic Telegraph*, printed at Cincinnati, of the building, altar, &c. By the way the altar is of stone, but they tell us this is only temporary, and will soon be superseded by a superb marble altar which is hourly expected from *Italy*. Why go all the way to Italy for an altar? Why not employ our own mechanics and artists? We have marble enough here, and men enough. But I suppose it is a *present*. Our country is receiving a great many presents now from abroad. Foreign *Catholics* are particularly kind to us. You know we are making the great experiment whether a free, representative government can sustain itself; and our Austrian and *Italian* brethren, sympathizing with us, want to help us all they can. They mourn especially over the deplorable lack of religion in this country, and are anxious to supply it. Nor is it in building and furnishing churches alone that they are disposed to help us. They cannot bear to see our children growing up in such ignorance. They are not used (they would have us believe) to an ignorant population; and then, what is to become of the republic if the people are not educated? So they come from Ireland, France, Italy, and all those countries, male and female, to educate us. A skeptical person might be tempted to ask if there is nothing of the kind to be done at home – if, for example, they cannot find any uneducated children in *Ireland,* but they must come over here to find them. However that be, they come. But what strikes me with wonder, is, that when they get here, they are all for educating *Protestant* children. Why do they not give the children of Catholics, their own people, a chance? There are many of them scattered over the land, and they are not all self-taught. I should like to have this explained. Common sense suggests that there must be a motive for making this distinction, and shrewdly suspects it is *proselytism.* Charity waits to hear if any more creditable reason can be assigned. But this is digression.

Well, on the 26th of October the grand building was consecrated. The procession consisted of an "ecclesiastical corps" amounting to fifty or sixty, of whom four were bishops, and twenty-eight priests, *twelve of whom were from twelve different nations.* You see they are coming upon us from all quarters. It would really seem as if all Europe was conspiring to pour in its priests among us. Here are priests of twelve different nations met at St. Louis! Protestantism has to depend for its men and money on native Americans; but Popery, you perceive, has all Europe to draw upon. If, with this advantage, the latter religion should make considerable progress in our country, we must not be surprised. Whether this influx of foreign priests augurs good or evil to our free institutions, is a question on which I will express no opinion.

I come now to the novelty which suggested the title of this article – the new discovery – the improvement I spoke of. The editor, or his correspondent, says, "As soon as the procession was organized, the pealing of three large and clear-sounding bells, and the thunder of two pieces of artillery, raised all hearts, as well as our own, to the Great and Almighty Being."

Now is not this something *new?* I always thought bells were to call people together, not to raise them up. But here he says they raised all hearts. However, it was with the help of the thundering artillery. It was the bells and guns together that did it. They made such a noise that at once all hearts were raised. What an effect from such a cause! Will the reader please to consider what was done and what did it? All hearts were raised to God by means of three bells and two guns! Is not this a *new* method of exciting devotion? Who ever heard before of noise composing the mind and preparing it for devout exercises? According to this, the fourth of July should be the day of all others in the year most favorable to devotion. And what a calamity deafness now appears to be; and how to be pitied they are who lived before the invention of gun powder! I never knew before that this was among the benefits of that invention, that it inspires devotional feelings, and raises hearts on high. But we must live and learn.

Well, all hearts being raised as before, "the holy relics [alias, the old bones] were moved towards the new habitation, where they shall enjoy anticipated resurrection – the presence of their God in his holy tabernacle." What this means, the reader must find out for himself. Now, when the relics were moved, the writer tells us what the guns did. "The guns fired a second salute." They could not contain themselves. Neither could the writer. "We felt," says he, "as if the soul of St. Louis was in the sound." A soul in a sound! Here is more that is new.

Then we are told who preached the dedication sermon; and afterwards we are informed, for our edification, that "during the divine sacrifice [the Protestant reader, perhaps, does not know what is meant by this phrase, but if the twelve nations continue to send over their priests, we shall know all about it by and by], two of the military stood with drawn swords, one at each side of the altar; they belonged to a guard of honor, formed expressly for the occasion. Besides whom, there were detachments from the four militia companies of the city, the Marions, the Greys, the Riflemen, and the Can Cannoniers from Jefferson Barracks, stationed at convenient

246 THOUGHTS ON POPERY

distances around the church." The reader will not forget that certain professed ambassadors of "the Prince of Peace" were here engaged in dedicating a church to his service; and this is the way they took to do it. If they had been consecrating a temple to *Mars,* I don't know how they could have selected more appropriate ceremonies. Here were soldiers, drawn swords, guns, and, as we shall see presently, colors and drums too, all to dedicate a church to the meek and lowly Jesus, and that too on the day of *rest!*

One more quotation from this glowing description. "When the solemn moment of the consecration approached, and the Son of the living God was going to descend, for the first time, into the new residence of his glory on earth, the drums beat the reveille, three of the star-spangled banners were lowered over the balustrade of the sanctuary, the artillery gave a deafening discharge." All that seems to have been wanting here was *three cheers.* Those would have been quite as suitable as the other accompaniments of the service. Reader, is this religion; and are these the things which are pleasing to God?

I have a word to say about the star-spangled banner. That is an ensign endeared to every American heart. Whether it is as highly esteemed by the *twelve* nations, I cannot say. But a church is not its appropriate place. There is another banner which should wave there – and that is not *star-spangled.* One solitary star distinguishes it – the star – the star of Bethlehem. Let us keep these things separate: under the one, go to fight the bloodless battles of our Lord – under the other, march to meet our country's foes. This is the doctrine of American Protestantism – no union of church and state, and no interchange of their appropriate banners.

THE END.

www.ingramcontent.com/pod-product-compliance
Lightning Source LLC
LaVergne TN
LVHW051501080426
835509LV00017B/1860